Simple Pleasures

Simple Pleasures

Soothing Suggestions & Small Comforts
for Living Well Year Round

Robert Taylor   Susannah Seton   David Greer

CONARI PRESS
Berkeley, CA

To all those who shared their pleasures:

Suzanne Albertson, Timothy Anderson, Joan Backus, Ame Beanland, Barbara Black, Kathie Brezer, Rick Brezer, Jennifer Brontsema, Adrien Brown, Daryl Brown, Terry Brumby, Rebecca Crichton, Ann Marie Cunningham, Esther Dick, Candas Dorsey, Dorothy Field, Derek Fox, Viola Fox, Sarah Gee, Will Glennon, Sue Hara, Kathleen Harper, Brian Harvey, Sarah Harvey, Larry Hunnicutt, Mags Johnston, Debby Jones, Eric Jones, Victoria Kahn, Brenda Knight, Ira Kurlander, Daniel Leen, Mollie MacGregor-Greer, Alison MacKenzie, Meg Mann, Laura Marceau, James Mays, Brian McDonald, Christina McKnight, Lynn Milnes, Patrick Pothier, Chris Roberts, Jim Roberts, Kevin Ronneseth, Raymond Rosenkranz, Gloria, Vincent, and Mary Jane Ryan, Eunice Scarfe, Fran Stevenson, Lisa Stevenson, Jill Swartz, Bonnie Thompson, Nancy Turner, Joan Tuttle, Mutang Urud, Joanie Vance.

And especially to Heather Fox, the Queen of Comforts

Conari Press books are distributed by Publishers Group West

A few of the stories in this book were originally published in
Slowing Down in a Speeded Up World, copyright 1994 by Adair Lara.
Reprinted by permission of Conari Press.

Cover illustration: Rae Ecklund
Cover and book design: Suzanne Albertson
Page 106 illustration: Jonathan Robertson

ISBN: 1-57324-075-3

Library of Congress Cataloging-in-Publication data

Taylor, Robert, 1940 June 1–
    Simple pleasures : soothing suggestions & small comforts for living well
year round / Robert Taylor & Susannah Seton & David Greer.
            p.   cm.
    ISBN 1-57324-075-3
    1. Simplicity.   2. Taylor, Robert, 1940 June 1– .   3. Pleasure.   I. Seton,
Susannah, 1952– .   II. Greer, David, 1946– .   III. Title.
BJ1496.T39   1997   96-44712
646.7dc—21   CIP

Printed in the United States of America on recycled paper
10 9 8 7

"I open the door. The gorgeous guest from afar sweeps in. In her hands are her gifts—the gifts of hours and farseeing moments, the gifts of mornings and evenings, the gift of spring and summer, the gift of autumn and winter. She must have searched the heavens for boons so rare."

—Abbie Graham

Simple Pleasures

A Potpourri of Pleasures

"When we lack proper time for the simple pleasures of life, for the enjoyment of eating, drinking, playing, creating, visiting friends, and watching children at play, then we have missed the purpose of life. Not on bread alone do we live but on all these human and heart-hungry luxuries."

—Ed Hayes

THERE'S A ZEN STORY ABOUT A MONK who was climbing a steep mountain. Suddenly there appeared above him a snarling tiger, blocking his path. Below him, the cliff fell away to a gaping chasm. While he was deciding what to do next, the monk turned his gaze to the mountainside in front of his face. There his eye fell upon a little plant that had managed to root itself in a crevice. And from the plant's single stem hung a perfect wild strawberry, ripe and red and glistening with dew. The monk reached out his hand, plucked the tiny fruit, pressed it against his tongue, and closed his eyes in ecstasy.

This book is about seizing the day and savoring the moment. It's about finding a touch of bliss in everyday events. And it's about paying attention to wild strawberries, whatever form they may take.

While most people would gladly agree that the pursuit of happiness is high on their list of priorities in life, they might think twice about saying the same about the pursuit of pleasure. In a culture that places so much emphasis on productivity, pleasure gets bad press. Somehow we associate it with idleness and decadence. But happiness, that elusive butterfly, has a lot to do with our ability to take delight in the day-to-day pleasures of our existence, whether that means the smell of a rose or the love felt for a child or the comforting rituals that soothe us. Too many of us pass these basic satisfactions by in the rush and clutter of modern life. And sometime later, whatever our grand achievements, like Citizen Kane we often long for a simpler life and remember best our Rosebuds, those small delights that seemed like nothing much at the time and brought us happiness when we thought about it least.

The simple pleasures of our lives are too important to be reduced to memories. They contribute to our physical and emotional health, and they even make us more "productive" by increasing our contentment. Whatever our situation, they're right at hand, if we only take the time to enjoy them. The grass may be greener on the other side, but a single flower that thrusts up through a crack in concrete can give as much delight as a whole meadow, if only we let it.

The people who seem to be most content don't focus on a time years ahead when they hope to have whatever they imagine it takes to be happy—money or time or a wonderful relationship. They live in the present and take their pleasure seriously. And they create their own pleasures.

We decided that the best way to create a book about simple pleasures was to ask people to tell us about the small delights in their lives. Some people talked about pleasures that they enjoy over and over, like the little girl who told us without hesitation that her greatest pleasure is "having my Dad rub my back with the palm of his finger." Others told of isolated moments of intense pleasure that kept coming back in their memories—an emotional chance reunion with a family long gone but not forgotten, the incredible sense of well-being after a prolonged illness. Still others talked of soothing comforts in their lives—ranging from hot water bottles and special foods to the cherished constancy of a special friend.

Some people not only talked about their pleasures but gave us instructions for creating them. That led to an idea that grew, and now the book is packed with recipes for comfort foods, both healthy and outrageously decadent, to satisfy every conceivable palate—recipes such as chocolate chip cookies and garlic soup and sun tea and jalapeño corn bread. You'll also find tips for making your own massage oils, foot lotions, potpourri and many other simple sensual delights. And garden tips and kitchen tips and things to do for fun, like tractor tracks in the snow and the dictionary game.

Finally, we added a sprinkling of quotes from many centuries and many places. The reason certain quotations survive in people's memories is that they have a way of capturing the essence of an

xiii

experience or feeling, so you find yourself saying, "That's exactly it!"

We believe that the secret of happiness in today's helter-skelter technological world is to learn how to enjoy less than we can afford. We need to rediscover the pleasures our grandparents knew when life was quieter and slower, when children without TVs knew how to amuse themselves, when pleasures were made, not bought—and enjoyed all the more because of it. We hope you'll remember many of the simple pleasures in your life that you may have drifted away from, and come away with many ideas for adding new pleasures into your life.

David Greer

Spring

Lilacs in dooryards
Holding quiet conversations with an early moon.

—Amy Lowell

Home

"April prepares her green traffic light and the world thinks Go."

—Christopher Morley

Home

A Job Well Done

I'm a window cleaner and I get very attached to the windows I work on. I know their individual personalities, their mineral deposits, bad seals, and BB holes. I remove every speck of bee gunk, snail trail, fly crud, and bird doo that desecrates "my" windows, as well as the damage inflicted by that natural enemy, the painter. I bring garden clippers and prune bushes and plants that dare to interfere with my windows. As I drive my route, I get great enjoyment from seeing my glass glistening in the sunlight.

"We will have to give up taking things for granted, even the apparently simple things."

—J.D. Bernal

Healthier Cleaning Pleasures

When the weather starts getting warmer and the days longer, you know it's time for a good spring cleaning. There's great satisfaction in a major cleaning project, but the result should be a clean-smelling house or apartment, not one overwhelmed with chemicals or artificial scents of some mythical forest glade. How many plastic containers of chemical spray cleaners do you need under the sink, anyway? They aren't good for you or the environment. Fortunately, nontoxic cleaning substitutes are within easy reach.

Baking soda is a mild cleanser for kitchen and bath fixtures; just sprinkle it straight from the box onto a damp cloth or sponge. A couple of tablespoons dissolved in a quart of water can be used to wash the interiors of refrigerators and freezers, neutralizing odors. Add a tablespoon to coffee pots and vacuum bottles, then fill them with water to freshen them, too. Still on supermarket shelves, venerable Bon Ami cleanser (with the drawing of the chick that "hasn't scratched yet") is a little more effective than baking soda, and doesn't contain chlorine, phosphates, perfumes, or harsh abrasives.

Borax or baking soda with lemon juice will handle soap film in the bathtub and shower. Adding a couple of teaspoons of vinegar to a quart of water produces a handy glass cleaner, and there's even a less pungent solution for the dishwasher—equal parts of borax and washing soda (sodium carbonate, often labeled as "detergent booster"). Discolored copper pots? Try a cleanser from early in the twentieth century: a tablespoon of salt mixed with a half-cup of vinegar.

There are also all-natural air fresheners made from the concentrated oils and essences of orange peels that can neutralize odors, not just cover them up. Orange-based fresheners are available in hardware and larger natural-food stores. Cedar oil spray can freshen pet beds and closets and renew the scent of cedar chests and shoe trees. And, for more than a century, Mrs. Stewart's Liquid Bluing has been added to the laundry rinse water to whiten sheets, shirts, and other fabrics that have yellowed or grayed with age. Mrs. Stewart—whose no-nonsense portrait is still on the label—would be pleased that she's still teaching us a thing or two about housekeeping.

5

Home

$\mathscr{P}$*sychic* $\mathscr{C}$*leanup*

When I accumulate too many people, experiences, and fatigue in my life, I get emotionally and spiritually disheveled. The sign that this is happening is that I have a dream full of cluttered, kaleidoscopic images. Then I know I need to set aside a day for a good old-fashioned clear-out. When I wake up on the appointed morning, I go on a cleaning binge in my trailer. I put away books and tidy up papers, empty the old cream cheese out of the fridge, and wash my clothes. I clean up my body, too, by drinking only juice and maybe going for a very long run. I unplug the phone, keep the radio turned off (news is clutter), and if anyone comes to visit me, I say, "I'm sorry, I'm not talking to anyone today."

At night, the clean-up ends when I go to bed in fresh, clean sheets and read something peaceful and uplifting. Then I have a good long sleep, free of cluttered dreams. The next day I feel completely replenished, with all my psychic garbage hauled away.

"What a gift of grace to be able to take the chaos from within and from it create some semblance of order."

—Katherine Paterson

THINGS TO DO

"Scent"sational Idea

Take your favorite essential oil (peach, rose, and vanilla are very nice environmental scents) and rub it on the light bulbs in your bedroom and the night light in the bathroom. The room will be infused with scent as light heats up the oil. For a "higher tech" approach, you can also buy inexpensive clay light bulb rings that hold the oil. Good sources for the oils, as well as all kinds of other yummy simple pleasures are: Body Time catalog and stores (510-524-0360), The Body Shop catalog and stores (800-541-2535), Bare Escentuals catalog and stores (800-227-3990), Cost Plus stores, Earthsake stores, Green World

Mercantile (415-771-5717), Red Rose catalog and stores (800-374-5505), and Hearthsong catalog and stores (800-432-6314).

"We should all just smell well and enjoy ourselves more."

—Cary Grant

The Zen of Vacuuming

I never wear shoes unless I have to. I always go barefoot if I'm painting or cooking. I like to feel the ground against my skin, with no interruption in the energy that comes through my feet. I prefer to live in the desert, where I don't need shoes either inside or outside. And wherever I'm living, clean floors are essential.

My love affair with vacuuming began when I was a child. The noise blocked out my mother's scolding, and I could feel like I was doing something that made grownups proud of me. Vacuuming is still my joy and meditation. I totally check out when I'm running my Electrolux over the floor. Sometimes I go over the same spot over and over again. I feel about my Electrolux the way some people feel about classic cars. It's like an old DeSoto or Studebaker. It never gets too old, it just keeps getting more stylish, and it gets the job done. The only thing better than walking barefoot on a freshly vacuumed floor is getting a foot massage.

7

Home

"That man is the richest whose pleasures are the cheapest."

—Thoreau

THINGS TO DO

If a foot rub is your idea of a good time, try doing it with peppermint foot lotion. Many people swear by it as the only curative for a long day's walk or a hard day of work (or shopping!). The Body Shop has a superior one. You can also make your own by adding 1 tablespoon of peppermint oil to 6 ounces of unscented lotion. Or try this therapeutic indulgence courtesy of the Fredericksburg Herb Farm in Fredericksburg, Texas: Grate approximately 1 cup of fresh ginger. Squeeze gently and add, along with a few drops of olive oil, to a foot basin or tub filled with hot water. Cover the bowl with a cloth or towel to preserve the heat, and soak for fifteen minutes. Then dry your feet and slip into a pair of warm socks.

Hanging Out the Wash

On Saturdays as soon as spring arrives, I take the sheets and undies outside into the fresh air and hang them up in the sun and wind. No one else is allowed the job—I tell them it's because they don't know how to hang out the clothes. I feel the early morning sun on my back and listen to quiet sounds as I leave the long week's raggedy days behind. I bathe in the morning light under the clothesline and delight in the feeling of air on my skin after being shut up in the office all week. When I bring the laundry in, I press my face to the sheets. They smell like all the promises that detergents make but don't keep; they smell like the very essence of spring.

Oh yes, I have a dryer, but on nice days it sits silent. Placed on the bed, the fragrant sheets from the line become a silent welcome after a tiring day.

> *"Smells are surer than sounds and sights to make the heartstrings crack."*
>
> —Rudyard Kipling

9

Home

THINGS TO DO

A Bird Haven

When the birds have begun to build their nests, that's the time to clean the lint screen in your dryer. Instead of throwing the lint away, put it out on a porch railing or even a branch of a tree. The birds will use it to line their homes.

"I was always a lover of soft-winged things."

—Victor Hugo

The Duct Tape Fan Club

If it ain't broke, don't fix it. That's a motto I can agree with, but I'd take it a step further—if it's broke, don't fix it with more than you need to. When things break, it's a pleasure to be able to fix them with whatever's close at hand, with minimal time and expense. People who share this philosophy usually swear allegiance to some universal solution for fixing things.

I've always been partial to duct tape. It doesn't matter if the broken item is a canoe or a computer or a chair, I'll always turn to duct tape first, and it's always a great satisfaction to find new uses for it. I've run into several other types of universal-solutions people who have tried unsuccessfully to convert me to their methods. There are the Krazy Glue people and the epoxy people and the minority group that favors little pieces of wire. Finally, there's the tiny fringe group that goes in for a mixture of glue and duct tape and wire. These are the desperate people who couldn't fix anything if their life depended on it. You can tell which group you're in by what you reach for in a crisis.

10

"What a people—we make something out of nothing and revel in its simple delicacy."

—Carol Talbot

THINGS TO DO

Instant Room Makeover

If you are tired of the way your living room or bedroom looks, do an instant makeover by revitalizing old throw pillows. Place a pillow kitty-cornered on top of a pretty scarf or bandanna. Bring opposing corners of the scarf or bandanna together and tie them in a knot. Do the same to the other corners. You have a new, colorful look for your home.

11

Home

Bear Essentials

I make teddy bears and the best part is right at the end when I sculpt a face on the bear. I never know till I've finished stuffing the bear what its personality is going to be. Something about the way the fur lies gives me my clue, and I go to work. Usually teddy bears have a worried, poignant expression that shows how empathic they are, but now and then they get a wild gleam in their eye and a foolish leer on their face. You just never know. Their sex is also a mystery until the very end, and sometimes remains so. I once dressed one of my bears as a boy, and it took me weeks to realize he'd be more comfortable in a dress. I'm still not sure if he was a girl or a transvestite.

"Simple pleasures are the last refuge of the complex."

—Oscar Wilde

12

THINGS TO DO

As the weather begins to warm and you no longer use the fireplace, evoke the romance and beauty of a fire by placing four or five pillar candles inside it. The soft light they will give off will compensate for the loss of the roaring fire.

Garden and the Great Outdoors

"The cherry tomato is a wonderful invention, producing,
as it does, a satisfactorily explosive squish when bitten."

—Miss Manners

13

Garden and the
Great Outdoors

Garden Surprises

Every spring I make a trip to the nursery to load up on puny little plants that have no blooms. It's an act of faith, because half the time I have no idea what they'll look like. Then in summer, the color combinations in my garden come as a wonderful surprise, far better than if I'd planned them. Gardening in spring is life-affirming. The outcome is often less important than the promise of things to be, and the plants transforming in my flower beds remind me of the potential for growth in other areas of my life.

"Anticipate the good so that you may enjoy it."

—Ethiopian proverb

Confronting Reality

Very early in the morning, when the mist is on the lake, I go down the hill in my nightie with a cup of hot tea and a handful of cat crunchies for Minnesota Fats, who comes with me. We get into the dory (Fats takes the bow), and I row out into the middle of the lake and just float there, luxuriating in the peace and stillness. When we come back to the shore, Fats rests on the dock, and I drop my nightie and slip, naked and quiet, into the water. It's a wonderful sensation to swim in the mist when you can't see the edges of where you're going or where you've been, and the air and the water are the same temperature so there's no feeling of separation. When I start to feel chilly, I go back up the hill to the pleasure of a hot bath on the deck, and I warm up from my swim in preparation for work.

My colleagues can always tell when I've been early-morning mist swimming by the dreamy grin on my face that lasts most of the morning. When I hear people come back from a wonderful experience and say, "Oh, well, back to reality," I remember the lake and the mist and the stillness and I think to myself, who decides reality has to be drudgery instead of intense pleasure?

THINGS TO DO

Aromatherapy, au Naturel

Every time you pass a lilac bush or an iris or daffodils in flower, take the time to bury your face in the bloom. Lilacs have a sweet and heady scent, and irises are musky and erotic. Close your eyes, breathe deeply and imagine the fragrance passing all through your body.

15

Garden and the Great Outdoors

The Perfection of Peas

Now and then an entire row of peas germinates without the cats rolling in them. They're most beautiful when they're maybe an inch high, before they get all straggly. They're just so fat and round and perfect, like a row of green stars in the sky.

> *"What can your eye desire to see, your ears to hear, your mouth to take, or your nose to smell that is not to be had in a garden?"*

> —William Lawson

THINGS TO DO

Planting the Seed

Gardeners are by nature optimists, and if there's anything more therapeutic and satisfying than working in a garden, it's planting the seed of wonder in the mind of a child. There's a small investment in a packet of seeds or—for the most impatient children, grandchildren, or young neighbors—a half-dozen tiny plants in a plastic packet.

Remember playing with puppet-like snapdragons when you were a kid? It's not a lost art. Youngsters may also enjoy fast-growing, towering sunflowers, fuzzy lamb's ears, fragrant sweet peas, lavender, and mint. And with a strawberry in a pot in a sunny location, kids can have their gardening project and eat it, too.

Or help youngsters sprout seeds indoors. Fold a couple of paper towels together to form a strip as wide as the towel and a few inches high. Moisten and place inside a peanut butter jar or similar-size jar, forming a border at the base. Crumple and moisten another paper towel and stuff into the center. Carefully place seeds—beans are easy to grow and handle—between the folded paper and the glass. Keep moist, but not soaked—for several days as seeds germinate. Kids can watch roots and plants sprout. When plants reach above the jar and two sets of leaves have formed, transplant to pots of soil or into the ground.

THINGS TO DO

Reflected Glory

Martha Stewart is renowned for making beautiful things that are often complicated to do. However, sometimes she has an idea that is simplicity itself. One such suggestion we recently saw is to line the edges of a garden path with pure white stones, pebbles, shells. That way, when the sun sets, "they'll reflect the moonlight, showing you the way."

17

Garden and the Great Outdoors

Art for Mules

As an artist who works with handmade paper, sometimes I make something that's too big or confrontational for someone's living room. Then I have the problem of owning and storing it.

Recently I started designing works of art that I install in the woods and let return to nature. I made a paper flag from maté with cutout images of figures with vegetables growing out of their arms that I got in Mexico—offerings to the gods of corn and tomatoes and beans. I put the flag in my garden, and it gave new life to my crops as the garden began to absorb it back to earth. I also made a giant book, in the form of a teepee, with text that spoke to wild creatures of the woods. I made it large enough for me to sit in, and I installed it in the woods. The messages in the book were meant to be for the deer and the mice. I had no idea that my book would speak as well to the mules that came and ate it.

THINGS TO DO

18

These delectable treats are easy to create; use them on top of ice cream or cakes. Pick the flowers fresh in the early morning.

Candied Flowers

violet blossoms

rose petals

I or 2 egg whites, depending on how many flowers you use

superfine sugar, to taste

Gently wash flowers and pat dry with a clean towel. Beat the egg whites in a small bowl. Pour the sugar into another bowl. Carefully dip the flowers into the egg whites, then roll in sugar, being sure to cover all sides. Set flowers on a cookie sheet and allow to dry in a warm place. Store in a flat container with waxed paper between layers. These will last for several days.

The Urge for Going

Every spring I get hit with the urge for going. It doesn't matter how—it could be by canoe or truck or plane—and the destination matters even less. For me, it's the most liberating experience to get up and go with no idea where I'm going to end up. It's about having no fear, no expectations, no obligations. I don't have to be anyone for anyone, and I'm open to meeting anyone and everyone. It's one of the few times when I feel there's no separation between me and life.

"Following the sun we left the old world."

—Inscription on one of
Columbus' ships

19

*Garden and the
Great Outdoors*

The Taste of Rain

In early spring, I like to catch on my tongue the drops of rain suspended from branches on trees and bushes. The best are witch hazel catkins, which have phenomenal small perfumed droplets—or so my imagination tells me. And the drops that hang from the red berries of hawthorns seem to carry inside them the reflection of the whole upside-down world. I also consider myself lucky if the night has brought a freezing rain that coats each twig in an icy casing. Then I do what deer do and chew on them, no hands. The clear, glittering ice on a twig is far better than any popsicle I ever tasted.

"We do not remember days, we remember moments."

—Cesare Pavese

THINGS TO DO

Heavy snowfalls are blessings for people who love their maple candy. The good news is that you don't need an acre of sugar maples and a bucket of sap to make it. A bottle of maple syrup will do just fine.

Maple Candy

1/2 cup maple syrup
1 baking pan full of packed, clean snow

Leave the pan of snow outside or in the fridge till the moment you're ready to use it. Then heat the maple syrup in a pot to 270 degrees (check with a candy thermometer). Carefully dribble the hot syrup in small patches over the snow. Each one of these patches will magically and immediately turn to chewy toffee that will amaze and delight your friends. That's all there is to it.

We've already said you don't need a sugar bush for this. Truth to tell, you don't even need snow. You can get the same result with crushed ice, if your fridge makes it.

Body and Soul

*"Modern beings have forgotten their beautiful and simple
natures. The only way to live is by living fully. We
should create our lives into a festival of growth and permanent creation."*

—Chamalú, a Wuechua
Indian mystic

21

Body and Soul

Why Pianists Don't Give Up

A Chopin prelude may be only a minute long, but I might spend
six months working on it, and it still gets away from me. Sometimes
when this happens, I let it sit for a week, without practicing at all.
And then one day I sit down at the piano and it's there. Without
being forced, without straining, the piece just appears under my fingers—a perfect, fleeting gem. That happy moment of discovery is
worth the months of searching.

*"Whenever I play, I throw myself away. It doesn't matter
where I am. I close my eyes and leave this earth."*

—Mary Lou Williams,
jazz pianist

THINGS TO DO

Your Own Perfume

With essential oils, you can create your own perfume, based on your mood at the time. All you need is an eyedropper and a variety of oils. Kimberley D. Wheat, buyer for Bare Escentuals, offers her favorite secret recipe; she calls it "Little Black Dress": 2 drops ylang ylang, 1 drop patchouli, and 1 drop bergamot added to 1 teaspoon jojoba oil. "Apply to pulse points!" Remember, essential oils are to be used only externally. Be sure not to ingest them; they can be toxic or even fatal. Be sure to keep them out of the reach of children, and test each one on a spot on your arm before you use them liberally in baths or as perfumes.

Dressing for Bed and Breakfast

I used to read magazine articles by mothers on how to save time. One of the tricks was to bathe the kids at night and then dress them for bed in shorts and a t-shirt so they'd be ready to go in the morning. Now when I go to bed, I often dress myself for the next day in a T-shirt and my long, cotton, wrinkle-proof skirt with the latticed waist and the material that stretches down to my ankles. When I do this, I think of those mothers. It's such a pleasure to get up in the morning and stay in my bed clothes, and it feels so good to walk to the store for milk without even bothering to get dressed.

> *"Life, within doors, has fewer pleasanter prospects than a*
> *neatly arranged and well-provisioned breakfast table."*

—Nathaniel Hawthorne

ℋegel at 𝒟awn

When I was doing my doctorate on Hegel, I once woke up at three in the morning, and went to an all-night restaurant. For reading material I decided to take along a volume of Hegel. Much to my surprise, it was all much clearer and more plausible than it had ever seemed in the daytime—perhaps because my mind in the hours before the dawn had not yet lapsed into its mundane ruts. Nowadays, one of my greatest pleasures is awakening very early in the morning and slowly savoring a few paragraphs from a choice philosophical treatise.

> *"Ink runs from the corners of my mouth.*
> *There is no happiness like mine.*
> *I have been eating poetry."*

—Mark Strand

23

Body and Soul

Cleaning Eye Glasses

Towards the end of the day, when I'm getting tired but still have a lot of work, I wash my face and clean my glasses, and then I'm good for another few hours. It's just a little ritual, but it leaves me feeling fresh and renewed, and I have the comfort of knowing my glasses won't slide down my nose. I also take pleasure in taking other people's glasses and cleaning them too.

24

THINGS TO DO

Natural Hair Care

A simple, effective, old-fashioned rinse is simply vinegar, preferably cider vinegar. Mix 2 tablespoons in 2 cups of warm water. Work through hair after shampooing and rinsing, then rinse again with clear water. For light hair, use lemon juice instead of vinegar. This will help restore the natural acid balance of the scalp and get rid of all traces of soap and shampoo.

For an all-purpose hair conditioner, combine 3/4 cup olive oil, 1/2 cup honey, and the juice of 1 lemon. Rinse hair with water and towel dry. Work a small amount of conditioner into hair, comb through and cover with a shower cap or plastic wrap for 1/2 hour. Shampoo and rinse thoroughly. Store remaining conditioner in the refrigerator.

The Artist's Journal

I have a journal in my studio in which I paint and write and break every artistic rule. I don't say, "I must never do this," I just put down whatever comes out of my head. Sometimes I think what I'm doing is brilliant, but it doesn't matter, since no one ever has to see it or judge it—I don't have to read what someone says about it in the paper. When I'm expressing myself in my journal, I feel drunk with color and material.

> *"The greatest part of our happiness and misery depends on our dispositions and not on our circumstances."*
>
> —Martha Washington

25

Body and Soul

THINGS TO DO

Newsprint Roll-Ends

If you feel the urge to express yourself in a big way, or if your paint-crazed child is constantly running out of paper, pay a visit to your local newspaper and ask if they have any roll-ends for sale. Newsprint comes in gigantic rolls that are often discarded when they're close to being used up. You can get them for a song (cheap) or, if you get lucky, for a smile (free).

The End of an Illness

There is nothing more wonderful than the first day after a long illness (in my case several years); when you walk down the street and feel well, the lightness is wonderful. So is the first moment of unsolicited well-being, not reactive but gratuitous. When you're recovering from a chronic or long-term sickness, you can summon the energy for reactive well-being long before you have any of those free-floating bursts of simple joie de vivre. They are the last thing to return as health returns.

> *"Is it so small a thing*
> *to have enjoy'd the sun,*
> *To have lived light in the spring,*
> *To have loved, to have thought, to have done?"*

—Matthew Arnold

THINGS TO DO

A Spring Tonic

Cultures throughout the world swear by garlic soup as a spring tonic and all-around cure for that under-the-weather feeling. No one knows if it is merely the pleasure in the taste that is the pick-me-up, or whether garlic has mysterious health properties. But give it a try when you're feeling blue and see if it works for you. Don't let the huge quantity of garlic scare you off—when cooked it turns very mellow.

Garlic Soup

4 heads of garlic

1 bunch parsley or thyme or marjoram, tied into a bundle
with string

1 quart chicken broth, vegetable broth, or water

juice of 1 lemon or lime

salt and pepper to taste

lightly toasted bread or croutons (optional)

27

Body and Soul

  Break up the heads of garlic into cloves, and discard the papery membrane, but don't peel the cloves, and place in a 4-quart soup pot with the herbs. Add the broth or water, cover and bring to a boil. Lower the heat and simmer for about 30 minutes, until garlic is very soft.

  Strain the soup through the fine disk of a food mill or puree in a blender or food processor, and push through a medium-mesh strainer with the back of a ladle. Add the lemon or lime juice, salt and pepper, and bread if desired. Serves 4.

The Perfect Backhand

The ball comes over the net to my left side, and I get in perfect position behind it and smash a low backhand that arcs into the opposite corner right by the service line. It's just the antidote I need for all the other backhands that go out of control, and I say to myself, Hey, I can do that—it's easy. It's like the pleasure of throwing a perfect spiral when I toss a football, and I notice how little effort it takes. I wouldn't enjoy it half as much if I could do it all the time.

"A little of what you fancy does you good."

—Marie Lloyd

THINGS TO DO

In Your Mind's Eye

Pollyanna and Dr. Norman Vincent Peale were right: Research shows that optimism and the power of positive thinking can affect everything from health to job success and life span. Several researchers have reported that pessimists who tend to blame themselves for their misfortunes are more susceptible to disease. The pessimist's typical attitude of helplessness may be associated with weakening of the immune system's resistance. Or pessimists may simply neglect their health.

A psychologist at the University of Pennsylvania, Martin Seligman, suggested that our initial, automatic reactions to minor misfortune can be self-defeating. The technique of "cognitive therapy" involves identifying these automatic, negative thoughts and replacing them with ones that are more realistic.

And who knew better than Dr. Norman Vincent Peale? His wife Ruth, that's who. In the 1950s, Peale was dissatisfied with his manuscript for a book, then called *The Power of Faith*, and threw it in the trash. His wife retrieved it and took it to a New York publisher, where an editor changed the word "faith" to "positive thinking." The result: ninety-eight weeks as America's best-selling nonfiction book, and an inspiration for generations.

So if you catch yourself saying things like "I know this won't turn out well," "I'm sure he's going to disappoint me," etc., try replacing them with thoughts like, "I'm going to do by best to make it come out well." You'll be giving your body and soul a boost!

29

Body and Soul

Animal Crackers

I'm a forty-year-old lawyer who goes looking for animal crackers whenever my day gets too stressful. They're the perfect size and shape for eating in one quick bite, they melt in my mouth, and they're sweet, but not too. But more than that, they take me back to my childhood, when life wasn't complicated, I didn't have difficult choices to make, and all I wanted was animal crackers and Mommy. I guess that's why animal crackers are so comforting to me now. When I was much younger, I used to talk to the animals, but now I just bite off their heads. My favorite is the gorilla, who looks like a very contented Buddha.

30

"Animal crackers and cocoa to drink,
That is the finest of suppers, I think;
When I'm grown up and can have what I please
I think I shall always insist upon these."

—Christopher Morley

THINGS TO DO

Melting Away Stress

If you're a very important attorney—or a very unimportant one—you can nibble on animal crackers at your desk all day, coaxing out those little bits from the box that looks like a miniature circus animal car. That woven string handle is so you can carry it outside your briefcase. And if you are a lawyer with a social conscience, look for Endangered Species animal crackers. Every time someone asks you for one, you can give them a little lecture about how the real animals need to be saved, not eaten.

If that doesn't appeal to you, you can recall another childhood pleasure with these easy-to-make brownies. They can furnish a week's worth of lunch bag treats, or disappear in a day or two with coffee or a big glass of milk. Thanks, Mom.

Nostalgic Brownies

2 ounces unsweetened chocolate

¼ cup butter

1 cup sugar

1 egg

1 teaspoon vanilla

½ cup all-purpose flour

pinch of salt

½ cup walnuts, broken into pieces or chopped

Preheat the oven to 300 degrees. Butter an 8-inch square baking pan, and line it with baking parchment or waxed paper. Butter and flour the waxed paper.

Melt the chocolate and butter in a saucepan over low heat. Remove from heat, stir well, then lightly stir in the sugar, egg, vanilla, flour, salt, and nuts.

Spread into the pan and bake for about 30 minutes, until center is set. Do not overbake, or brownies will lose their chewy texture and become dry.

31

Body and Soul

Remove pan from the oven and cool on a rack about 5 minutes. Turn out onto the rack and peel off the paper. While still warm, cut into squares with a greased knife. Makes 16 brownies.

Whatever the seasoning, whatever the dish, whatever the
occasion, do it generously and with love,
for that in the end is what the shared experience of
cooking and eating is all about.

—Elizabeth Rozin

Family and Friends

'Tis the gift to be simple . . .

—Shaker song

33

Friends and Family

Desert Hoops

An old man in Chile once told me about a simple pleasure he and his sister invented for themselves when they were children. They lived in an isolated house far out in a flat and windy desert. Some mornings when they were bored and had nothing to do, they would make hoops out of brightly colored paper and place them on edge on the desert sand. The wind would roll the away, and the children would watch them disappear towards the horizon. At midday, when the wind reversed its direction, the children would watch for tiny colored specks in the distance—the hoops were coming back, careening past the house towards the opposite horizon. Sometimes the boy and his sister would make hoops for several days in succession, setting up a brilliant multicolored traffic of wheels across the barren land.

"I said to the Wanting Creature inside of me, 'What is
this river you want to cross? Do you believe that there is
some other place that will make the soul less thirsty? In
that great absence you will find nothing. What we seek is
here already . . . Just throw away all thoughts of imaginary things not yet come and stand firm in that which
you are.'"

—Kabir

THINGS TO DO

Homemade Play Dough

This preschool staple is easy to make in batches at home.
It's worth keeping an assortment of bottled food coloring for
projects like these, even if you don't use them often for cooking.

1 cup salt

1¼ cups water

2 teaspoons vegetable oil

3 cups all-purpose flour (not self-rising)

2 tablespoons cornstarch

Food coloring

In a large bowl, mix salt, water and vegetable oil. Continue
mixing while adding flour and cornstarch. Knead until smooth. If

dough seems too sticky, add a little flour. If too dry, add a little water.

Divide the dough into several lumps. Add a few drops of food coloring to each lump and knead to mix the color into the dough. Store in air-tight containers, for this will dry out if exposed to air.

Unselfconscious Contact

35

Friends and Family

Children are such heavy sleepers that you can lean over them and nuzzle and pat them without waking them up. Sometimes I'll breathe in the scent of the shampoo on my son's hair and I'll think how extraordinary this little guy is and how lucky I am. When he wakes up, he puts out his arms to be carried and touches his little face to mine and says, "I love you Mommy" in that stream-of-consciousness way, where whatever he's thinking just comes out of his mouth. As adults, we're always aware of another person's reaction when we say something like that or touch him or her. I've never had such unselfconscious contact with anyone as I do with my boy. There's something so intimate about ministering to someone from the moment they're born that you never have to establish a relationship. It's already there, and the love just keeps on growing.

> *"The darn trouble with cleaning the house is it gets dirty
> the next day anyway. So skip a week if you have to.
> The children are the most important thing."*
>
> —Barbara Bush

THINGS TO DO

Do it Together

You and your family can make your own wrapping paper.
Buy a roll of white butcher paper or brown paper. For ease, you
can purchase a couple of rubber stamps and different colored
ink pads, and simply stamp out a pattern on your paper. Be careful not to smear it as you go. To make the paper even more personalized, you can make your own "rubber stamps." Cut a potato in half, then carve a simple shape into the center, then cut
the sides away so your center design is elevated enough to
make a clear impression. Try simple shapes like hearts, stars,
dots, and diamonds. For simple polka dots you can use wine
corks. What's great is that each person gets to express his or
her individuality.

Brand New Socks

My dad had two favorite expressions: "He who shoots first lives longest" and "The first one up is the one best dressed." We were a large family, and all the kids' socks were pooled, so if you got up late, you might not even get matching socks. I guess that's where my sock psychosis came from. I just love brand new socks. It's such a thrill breaking them out of the package, when they're soft and tight-fitting and they've never been inside a dirty old shoe. The first wash wrecks them. That's why I always set aside new socks for special occasions, such as traveling or a fancy dinner.

> *"Let your boat of life be light, packed with only what you need—a homely home and simple pleasures, one or two friends, worthy of the name, someone to love and to love you, a cat, a dog, a pipe or two, [and] enough to eat and enough to wear . . ."*

—Jerome K. Jerome

37

Friends and Family

Galloping

One of the greatest days of the year at boarding school was when we took the horses to the ocean for the first spring ride along the beach. They were tired of being cooped up all winter and were · eager to be out, and they ran fully open and wild on the sand. For me it was the delicious combination of fear and excitement that I didn't often experience, and I tried unsuccessfully each year not to smile as we did it, because we rode so fast that I always got sand in my braces.

"The path to your heart's desire is never overgrown."

—Kigezi proverb

THINGS TO DO

For Love of Books

If you are feeling like your head is full of fog and you haven't had an interesting conversation with anyone recently, consider joining or starting a book club. Many bookstores run several groups (and may even offer discounts if you all buy your books through the store), and community newsletters often run classifieds with groups looking for new members. Most groups we know are made up of friends who use the club as a way to get together on a regular basis. You need enough people to make it interesting and to accommodate the vagaries of people's vacation schedules, etc. Six to eight is a ballpark figure. Usually groups rotate who picks the book for the next meeting; some groups have page limits. Many book group guides now exist to help you pick books, provide discussion topics, and offer suggestions. Check with your local bookstore.

Nursing a Child

Nursing my baby is a source of exquisite pleasure in so many different ways. It's always awesome to me that I'm providing life to another being through the milk in my body. I delight in the feel of his soft head against my skin and the sight of milk dribbling from his mouth as he sucks. It's a great physical relief have him ease the pressure on my swollen breast, and it's a delight to see the joy in his little face as he looks up at me and touches my cheek or puts his fingers in my mouth—an ecstasy so complete it's like he's just had a shot of morphine. Finally, there's the pleasure I get from the smell of his baby skin and his fresh flannel clothes—a pleasure that lasts right up to the moment he pauses during his feeding to vomit all over the place.

"The great high of winning Wimbledon lasts for about a week. You go down in the record books, but you don't have anything tangible to hold on to. But having a baby—there just isn't any comparison."

—Chris Evert

39

Friends and Family

The Comfort Egg

When my second daughter was due to be born, the Jamaican

doctor I was seeing said to me, "Be sure and take time for the first child—the child who will feel displaced. In our country mothers make this time a ritual—an eating ritual. They spoonfeed a soft-boiled egg to the elder child every day. It's a small moment to make the child feel the center of attention again, it gives eye-to-eye contact, it provides a warm and soothing taste, and it guarantees time—one on one—for the older child."

I thought it was a great idea and when I did it, I found it was as wonderful for me as it was for my daughter. "Don't forget the comfort egg," I used to say to myself—and it was a comfort to me to have at least one moment ritualized in the chaos of those days.

Years later, when my youngest daughter—who was then 16—was crying inconsolably for her father, who had been killed some months before in a car accident, I could think of nothing to say in the presence of her pain. So I brought her milky tea and a soft-boiled egg which I fed to her myself with the buttered "toast soldiers" her father had always made, and stayed with her until the pain had somewhat—at least on this occasion—passed again.

*"What I love about cooking is that after a hard day,
there is something comforting about the fact that if you
melt butter and add flour and then hot stock, it will get
thick!"*

—Nora Ephron

THINGS TO DO

Comfort Food

Where are the comforting childhood favorites of yester-year? They're on the menu—at prices that would stun our grandmothers—at some of the trendiest restaurants. Casseroles that were the standard fare of budget cookbooks during the Depression of the 1930s, puddings created to disguise left-overs—they've made their way from humble supper to haute cuisine.

Which doesn't mean they aren't still comforting. Depending on your generation, these evocative foods could be Proust's madeleines, Franco-American canned spaghetti, Eskimo Pie ice cream sandwiches, or the sticky, syrupy apple dessert offered in the frozen dinners of the '50s and '60s.

Bread pudding may be the all-purpose comfort food that is easiest to reproduce. It has inspired everyone from Leon Lianides of New York's legendary Coach House restaurant to Marion Cunningham, who updated *The Fannie Farmer Cookbook*. (Cunningham pointed out that bread pudding was a "great paci-fier" for boarding school students for generations—sometimes the only decent dish in the dining hall.)

Bread and Butter Pudding

About 5 slices firm, slightly stale bread

Butter

41

Friends and Family

¼ cup raisins

3 eggs

2½ cups milk

¾ cup brown sugar, packed

½ teaspoon vanilla

Dash of salt

Nutmeg

Preheat oven to 350 degrees. Toast bread lightly, butter, and cut into cubes. There should be about 3 cups. Mix bread cubes and raisins in a buttered 1½-quart casserole.

Beat eggs, stir in milk. Strain into a bowl and stir in sugar, vanilla, and salt. Pour over bread and allow to stand 30 minutes for egg mixture to be absorbed. Sprinkle nutmeg on top.

Place casserole in a slightly larger, shallow pan in oven. Pour boiling water into outer pan to a depth of about 1 inch. Bake 45 minutes to an hour until custard is set. Serve warm. Makes 6 servings.

THINGS TO DO

Artistic Honor

Next time you host a party, create a piece of art for the guest of honor. Buy a simple canvas. Divide it into even sections using a pencil and ruler. Go over your pencil lines with permanent colored markers or paint. Provide guests with paints and brushes and have each person decorate a square. Your guest will have a colorful memento of the occasion. This works well for a variety of occasions: baby showers, housewarmings, high-school graduations, bon voyage . . .

> *"'How much are your yams?' I said, suddenly hungry.*
> *They ten cents and they sweet,' he said, his voice quaver-*
> *ing with age. . . . I took a bite, finding it as sweet and hot*
> *as any I'd ever had, and was overcome with such a surge*
> *of homesickness that I turned away to keep my control."*
>
> —Ralph Ellison

43

*Friends and
Family*

A Dog's Life

Whenever I take my golden retriever for a walk along the waterfront, I take great pleasure in watching him being in his body, completely unrestrained in his dogginess. Everything he does he does with intensity, whether it's walking into the ocean and gazing into the water, or smelling tree trunks (checking his pee-mail), or coming across something foul and looking up at me as if to say, "this is so good I just have to roll in it," or flopping down in total relaxation. It's satisfying to see him so happy in his environment, expressing himself so completely. We people are taught to hide what we feel, and we feel vulnerable if we show our pleasure too enthusiastically.

Walking with Newheart is a constant reminder to me to keep striving to live life fully and not hold myself back.

THINGS TO DO

Stuffed Kongs

If you have to leave your dog alone in the house and you'd like it to have a special treat while you're gone, buy a kong (a hollow bouncy dog toy, available at pet stores) and some Cheez Whiz or peanut butter. Squeeze a couple of spoonfuls of Cheez Whiz or peanut butter through the hole in the end of the kong. After you leave the house, the dog will stare out the window for a while, feeling mournful and cursing you silently. Once she discovers the kong, however, all will be forgiven. Imagine that every time your dog bites into her kong a little burst of Cheez Whiz oozes out and covers her snout. In dog terms, this is about as orgiastic as it gets. She'll be occupied for hours, trying to get her tongue in the hole. Variation: Insert a dog biscuit instead of cheese or peanut butter.

Gather Thee Rose Petals

When I was young, my brother and sister and I used to make May baskets for all the houses in the neighborhood to celebrate the

May Day. They were incredibly easy to make, and we would get such a thrill out of hanging them on front door knobs, then ringing the bell and running to a hiding spot where we would observe the face of the recipient. It was then I first learned the particular pleasure of anonymous giving. It's been a long time since I even thought about it, but the remembered pleasure is so strong, I think I'll do it with my kids this spring.

45

THINGS TO DO

May Baskets

Friends and Family

To make yourself or your neighbors a May basket, gather flowers (we always picked the first wildflowers of the season, but store-bought is okay too) and make them into an attractive bouquet. Tie the stems together with a rubber band. Moisten half a paper towel with water and wrap around the ends of the stem and then place a small plastic bag around the towel and tie with another rubber band. (This is to keep flowers fresh.) Set aside.

To make a cone basket, get a 8½ x 11-inch piece of construction paper. Hold the paper in two hands as if you were reading a letter. Turn slightly so that the left corner points down at you. This will be the bottom of the cone. Roll one side so that it is tighter at bottom and more open at top. Stick your hand in top to expand the top opening and at the same time tighten the point at the bottom. Staple or tape the outer flap. When you finish, it should look like an ice cream waffle cone.

To make the handle, simply cut a ½-inch wide strip from the long side of a 8½ x 11 inch piece of construction paper. Staple one end to each side of the cone. (You can also use ribbon or raffia if you wanted to.) Place flowers inside and you are ready to make your delivery!

Simple Treasures

Recently I was given a box of fabric by a friend whose mother-in-law had died at a great age. Nothing pleases me more than to receive gifts of fabric, but she apologized, saying the box had been hidden away in a closet and she didn't think there was anything useful in it. Perhaps she was right, but going through that box was one of the most pleasurable experiences I can recall.

It was filled with the thrift and care of a true saver. There were bits of underwear elastic rolled up tightly and pinned together. Strips of velvet. Curtain weights—little molten blobs of soft lead. A clutch of mother-of-pearl buttons sewn together. Good steel pins saved in a lozenge tin. Scarves saved from holidays, embossed with images of racetracks and Jamaican hotels. Woolen pants cuffs.

A bunch of wooden spools from Woolworth's with only an inch of thread clinging to each. Upholstery samples. A silk pincushion, leaking sawdust, that still held some nice glass-headed dressmaker's pins. A collection of clothing labels with fancy names like Belle-o'-the-Ball and Lady Splendid, held together with a tiny brass safety pin. A strand of baby hair, brittle now, in a tiny white envelope. Pockets long removed from jackets but folded together neatly in a bundle. One glove, the other long lost.

It went on and on, poignant scraps and leftovers, and I felt I knew her, could hear her sensible voice saying, "Well, someday this will come in handy." It never did, of course.

> *"The ordinary arts we practice every day at home are of more importance to the soul than their simplicity might suggest."*
>
> —Thomas Moore

47

Friends and Family

THINGS TO DO

Spring Fever Cures

When the kids have been cooped up in the house too long playing Nintendo and watching TV and have steam to let off, why not suggest that they round up the neighbor kids and try a batch of the games more popular in previous generations? You'll recognize them: Leap Frog; Hopscotch; King of the Hill; Duck, Duck Goose; Red Light; Mother May I; Simon Says; marbles, and jacks. Who says fun has to come in a box and cost $50 or more? Maybe they will entice you to join them in a trip down nostalgia lane.

Brief Pleasures

Not wearing my watch, and more importantly, not needing to.

The powerful scent of honeysuckle and magnolia wafting through dewy air at the dawning of a summer's day.

Driving fast through the mountains with the top down and powerful music blaring out of the speakers—the "Ode to Joy" or Janis Joplin.

Drifting off to sleep in the musty bedroom of an old lakeshore cottage to the drone of distant motorboats and the quiet lapping of waves.

The distant wail of a freight train whistle echoing in the mountains at night.

Waking up each morning at the age of eighty-two, knowing I'm living on borrowed time and savoring every moment of it.

A mouthful of watermelon on a sweltering day in a place where you can spit out the seeds as far as you want and let the juice dribble all down your chin and chest.

The intimacy of making and sharing food with dear friends at dinner.

Being wrapped in a hot flannel the moment after giving birth.

Hearing the Major 9th chord, properly placed in a tune, the way it is in Rita Coolidge's "Seven Bridges Road," so it resonates deeply within my soul and sends a thrill through my body.

49

The smell of a new rubber baby doll in my Christmas stocking when I was a child.

Remembering that there's dry clothing in a plastic bag at the bottom of your pack after you've dumped your canoe two days into a wilderness trip.

Telling a dream to someone who really wants to hear it, even though it makes no sense and sounds totally boring once you've woken up.

Having my dad rub my back with the palm of his finger.

Watching people from international flights arrive at the airport and greet their relatives they haven't seen for weeks or years.

Summer

It was a lovely day of blue skies and gentle breezes.
Bees buzzed, birds tootled, and squirrels bustled to and fro,
getting their sun-tan in the bright sunshine.
In a word all Nature smiled.

—P.G. Wodehouse

Home

"In cooking, as in all the arts, simplicity is the sign of perfection."

—Curnonsky

53

Home

Home Is Where the Car Is

When I flew into Montreal I called my friend from the airport. "I'll come and pick you up," she said.

"Don't bother," I said, "I've rented a car."

"What do you need a car for? All you're doing is driving downtown."

"I've become self-indulgent," I explained.

When I move from place to place, a car is like a room of my own, a postage stamp of a space that's mine alone. My parents were immigrants, and we never had a sense of place where we belonged. When I visited England, people took me for an American, but in the States we were Norwegians who never quite belonged. We get our sense of place from where we are, and if you feel like you don't belong where you are, there's nothing better than a car to give a sense of place. When I'm behind the wheel, I'm in charge. I fill the car with clothes and books, I don't have to worry about picking them up, and I'm not intruding on anyone else's space. It's all mine, wherever I am. That's why I rent a car.

> *"It isn't the great big pleasures that count the most; it's making a great deal out of the little ones."*
>
> —Jean Webster

54

A Yeasty Connection

I've been scanning the sales ads, thinking about getting a bread machine. Maybe if I wait awhile, I thought, I can get one cheaper. But then I remembered how I like to spank the dough to see if it is kneaded enough—as one book said, it should feel like a baby's bottom. That thought reminds me how connected I feel to countless generations of women who have made bread for their families, and how much I love the smell of bread baking.

I wonder how it would feel for that bread to come from a machine into which I dump ingredients in the rush of doing something else, then punch in the correct time-delay sequence. No more thinking of all the women who have made bread before me; no more smacking it to see if it feels like a baby's bottom.

On second thought, I think I'll keep the flour on the floor, the overactive yeast oozing out of the cup, and the awkward tiptoe position I have to assume to knead the bread on a counter that's too high. I'll keep it all, happily.

THINGS TO DO

Camping Bread

55

Nothing makes meals on a wilderness camping trip more memorable than good bread made on the spot. The following is an old standby of north Ontario canoeists.

Home

Bannock

3 cups white flour

½ cup soy flour

2 cup whole wheat flour

½ cup bran

½ cup wheat germ

2 tablespoons baking powder

1 teaspoon salt

⅔ cup powdered milk

⅔ cup shortening

2 cups water (approx.)

raisins, currants or cheddar cheese, to taste, optional

1 cut and peeled stick

Mix together the dry ingredients before you leave on your trip, and keep them in a waterproof container. When you're ready to cook the bannock, make a good campfire with lots of coals, and when it's close to being ready, mix up the dough. Work the shortening into the dry ingredients with your fingers, and add enough water to make a stiff dough that's still sticky enough to stay on the stick you have cut and peeled for the occasion. Knead in some raisins, currants, or cheddar cheese if you feel like giving the bannock some extra pizzazz. Then wrap dough around the stick and roast it over the hot coals. You'll know the bannock is close to done when it starts browning and drying out. Pull it off the stick and use it however you'd use bread. As in most campfire recipes, there's no absolute rules for doneness. You learn by trial and error and scraping off ashes.

The Moveable Feast

I can't cook. Because I am a woman and "supposed" to know how, I've decided to be horrible at it. Some weekends, though, I'm overcome by the desire to prepare a meal. A great meal.

I take all day. I imagine what the perfect meal would be—fresh, organic vegetables, wonderfully ripe fruit, a beautiful salad, maybe a light pasta, some freshly caught seafood . . . whatever. Then I plan my route. My favorite cheese counter is always a stop; I'll ask the man at the counter, "What do you recommend?" and he'll give me a taste of a new cheese from Denmark or Provence that makes me swoon, and I'll buy it.

Next I stop by the bakery. Usually a baguette is the perfect accouterment to go with my cheese, and right on the spot, I eat part of it to get me through the rest of my strenuous day. Then I go to my favorite corner produce stand and the health-food store. I load up on veggies and fruit, imagining all of the tastes in their various combinations. And finally I stop and buy a bottle of wine. A good Merlot.

When I get home, I unpack my groceries. I open the wine. I slice up my baguette and spread on the ripe cheese. I cut up the cantaloupe and garnish it with strawberries and purple grapes. The little organic pear-shaped tomatoes, along with an avocado, are thrown onto some crisp lettuce and then lightly misted with oil and vinegar, salt and pepper. And then I take my delectables to the couch, where my favorite book is waiting, and eat.

57

Home

THINGS TO DO

Put it on Ice

To make a striking presentation for shrimp salad or other cold dishes, make an ice bowl. Choose two bowls. One must be able to nest inside the other with about ½ to 1 inch of space in between. Fill the larger bowl with water and then place the other inside. Carefully place them in the freezer overnight. When you remove them from the freezer, if you have trouble removing the top bowl, pour a little warm water into it. (Don't get the water between the two bowls, it will make the ice start to melt.) If you have trouble getting the bottom bowl to separate from the ice, dip it into a sinkful, or large bowl full of warm water. You can make this even more special by freezing bits of parsley, lemon, or other fruit or herbs into the ice.

THINGS TO DO

Flower Salads

Several common flowers are edible—and add an element of color and surprise to an ordinary green salad. Not all flowers are edible, though, so make sure the ones you choose are, and wash and dry thoroughly before using. Common edibles include: nasturtiums, roses, borage, marigolds, squash flowers, and violets.

The Wonders of Water

I'm convinced that in a previous life I was a fish because there is something about water that gives me such comfort. When I was a kid, I grew up in a town in New England with a lake, and every day in the summer, my mother would take us there for the afternoon. I would lie for hours in the bathtub-temperature water, just floating, until my mother would say it was time to go home and I would reluctantly become bound by gravity again. These days, I take my water in whatever form I can get it—shower, tub, hot tub, swimming pool, hot springs, stream, pond—any place wet and warm (no shockingly cold immersion for me) in which I can empty my mind and loosen my ties to the earth. Nothing else I have ever experienced comes close to matching the ecstasy of weightlessness that water can give.

Even the sound of running or falling water has a soothing effect on me. My husband and I recently moved into a house with a small fish pond off the back deck. The pond has a tiny waterfall and a bubbling fountain and I find the gurgling of the water so pleasant that we're planning on building a matching pond on the other side of the deck.

59

Home

THINGS TO DO

Not everyone is fortunate to have easy access to a swimming hole (and there are even people who don't like being in water). But you can have the sound of running water no matter where you are. If you have even a small yard, you can create a pond for a surprisingly low cost. Good resources are Sunset's *Garden Pools, Fountains and Waterfalls* and Ortho's *Garden Pools and Fountains*. In addition, there are several catalogs offering indoor fountains, some even small enough for an office desk, including Art & Artifact (800-231-6766), Red Rose (800-220-ROSE), Whole Life Products (800-634-9057), Water Muse (800-898-2069), and Real Goods (800-762-7325).

If you are the handy type, you can make your own indoor fountain in less than an hour for around $75. This one is meant to be viewed from only three sides and you must have an electrical outlet nearby. The pump is available at most hardware stores.

Waterfall Fountain

1 glazed pottery basin, about 17" long x 12" wide x 4" high, without drainage holes

About 5-7 assorted clean, polished stones, small enough to fit in basin, but large enough to create a "mountain"

1 small electric recirculating pump

1 foot of clear plastic tubing

In the basin, arrange the stone asymmetrically to create a slope and stream bed, leaving enough room behind the mound to place the pump. Set the pump behind the stones and run the tubing from the pump up and over the back side of the stones, positioning the other end of the tube to allow the water to cascade gracefully over the rocks. Fill the basin with enough water to cover the pump. Plug in and add more water or adjust rocks to create the cascade you desire.

Traveling Heavy

I never travel without excess baggage. I love the comfort of having twice as much as I need. I do not consider it a virtue to travel to Europe with one backpack. And when I buy a book, I often get two copies—one for the bath and one for the bookshelf.

"Books are a delightful society. If you go into a room filled with books, even without taking them from their shelves, they seem to speak to you, to welcome you."

—William Gladstone

61

Home

THINGS TO DO

Grow or purchase a large quantity of lavender and throw it into a big bowl in your bathroom. Every time you shower, the warm, moist air will activate the scent of the lavender for a wonderful, calming bathroom treat.

Lavender is such a wonderful flower for cooking and decorating as well as bathing that you should consider making a long-term investment and plant a lavender bush. Every year it will grow large and give you dozens of blooms. Cut the stalks when the flowers are just past their peak. The stalks can be tied up with a ribbon for a beautiful dried flower wreath, and the crumbled flowers can be used to flavor all types of dishes.

A Vaseful of Joy

One of the little things I take true delight in on a regular basis is flower arranging. I am not good with my hands (my sister used to leave the house in fear when I was learning to sew in junior high), but I have the urge to make something beautiful, and over the years I have discovered that flower arranging is my creative medium. I don't spend a lot of money on it—I don't have fancy vases and don't buy exotic blooms. I work from whatever is blooming in my garden or whatever is selling for a couple dollars at the flower stand. At Christmas or Easter, I may splurge and spend as much as ten dollars. But usually it's just a few homegrown roses or roadside poppies or a sprig of holly from the tree in my yard. I have never read a book about the principles of flower arranging and I don't spend too much time on it—maybe five minutes at the most. For me, the joy comes from the ease with which it is possible to make something pleasing to look at: selecting an old yellow mustard jar, filling it with blue cornflowers and placing it on the kitchen table. Ongoing beauty, meal after meal, in only two minutes!

62

THINGS TO DO

Easy Potpourri

After your bouquet has had its day, cut off the tops of

flowers such as as roses, lavender, rose geranium, delphinium, and lemon verbena when they are fully opened, but before they fade. Spread on a rack, such as a cake rack, and let them dry in a warm but shady spot. This may take a week or longer—until the petals feel dry but have not turned brittle.

Spread a layer of petals about ½ inch deep in a container that can be sealed airtight. Sprinkle with a little salt and ½ teaspoon mixed spice such as cinnamon, cloves, mace, and allspice, plus some dried grated orange or lemon peel. Continue the layers until you've used all the flower petals. On the top, sprinkle a few drops of a perfume with a fragrance you like.

Store in a cool, dark place for about two weeks. Stir, reseal and store for six to eight weeks more, stirring once a week. Then place the potpourri in an attractive glass or ceramic jar that can be closed tightly. Open the jar to fill the room with fragrance; close it to preserve the potpourri. You can also package it up in a basket, with ribbons or raffia for gift-giving.

63

Home

Make Mine Iced

If I were to be really honest, I would have to confess that one of the greatest pleasures in my life is an ice-cold Coke (but only in a glass bottle, the ones in the can taste metallic) on a hot summer's day. The combination of the sweetness yet tanginess of the flavor with the amount of carbonation—nothing surpasses it. Apparently, I am not alone in my obsession, as confirmed by the enormous storm created when the company tried to introduce a new formula.

Unfortunately, I love Coke so much that I tend to overindulge (I once lost ten pounds just by cutting it out of my diet altogether) and have had to find other liquid refreshments. Enter iced tea: great tasting, lots of different flavors if that's what you desire, no carbonation (there's only so many bubbles a person can consume a day without feeling a bit overdone), no sugar and therefore no calories and, if you use decaf tea, absolutely not bad for you in any way. I drink it summer and winter, night and day. It is so satisfying that it makes me forget all about Coke. Well, almost.

64

> *"Tea, thou soft, thou sober, sage and venerable drink . . ."*
>
> —Colley Cibber

THINGS TO DO

Sun Tea

Sun tea is great because it has a mellower flavor than brewed tea. Drop four teabags in a quart pitcher of water (the pitcher must be glass). Cover to keep out bugs and put the pitcher outside in the full sun. After a couple of hours, when the sun is really hot and you are too, remove the teabags. Add ice and serve.

For a variation, use a peach fruit tea. When the tea is
ready, cut up a chilled peach into bite-sized pieces and add to
the tea. Serve immediately for a one-of-a-kind refresher.

Making Lists

I'm an obsessive list-maker. It's a simple way of feeling like I'm in
control, and it gives me a sense of what errands and tasks are man-
ageable. The best part is when enough things get crossed off and the
list gets messy and I can make a new list and assess my priorities all
over again. For a while I tried making lists on an electronic organiz-
er, but I finally gave up because I missed the satisfaction of running
my pencil through an item. It's just not the same with a Delete key.

65

Home

THINGS TO DO

Simple Summer Refreshers

Freeze little slices of lemon or lime into your ice cubes
for a pretty and refreshing touch in ice tea or other cold drinks.
You can also freeze orange or cranberry juice into ice cubes to
add sparkle to lemon-lime soda.

Garden and the Great Outdoors

"A garden is not for giving or taking. A garden is for all."

—F. H. Burnett

The Delights of Disorder

I thought all the poppies in my garden were pink opium poppies, but this year they were joined by a bunch of Hungarian poppies with translucent silk skirts like faded lavender. Another year we had a whole slew of crazy colored gourds come out of nowhere. Flowers and vegetables keep coming up that we haven't sown for years. This rampant volunteerism of plants popping up never ceases to amaze and delight me. When my sweet cicely got out of hand in my garden, I threw a bunch of it by the back fence, and it has prospered there ever since. This is my ultimate goal—to find the right place for every plant where it can run rampant and be happy and I don't have to do anything except lie in the hammock and watch the garden come back year after year however it wants.

"Earth laughs in flowers."

—Ralph Waldo Emerson

THINGS TO DO

Grow a yard of woolly thyme instead of grass. Not only is it easier to care for and (virtually) never needs watering, it will hold the heat of the day's sun and fill your yard with a singularly pleasing smell. At the very least, try it between the stones or bricks of your front walk or garden path. Every time you walk across it, the smell will waft up. (And you can use it in any recipe that calls for thyme.)

"Smell is a potent wizard that transports us across thousands of miles and all the years we have lived."

—Helen Keller

The Good Earth

When I go back for a visit to the family farm, I always take some time to head out to the summer-fallowed fields. Once I'm there, I lie down and press my face into the earth. The dirt is black and rich and cushiony, and smells like my grandmother did when she was big and I was just a little girl—dank and sweet and musty.

"Speak to the earth, and it shall teach thee."

—Job 12:8

THINGS TO DO

Pressed Flowers

Making pressed flowers is incredibly easy. It requires no special equipment and costs absolutely nothing. Here's how:

When your new telephone book comes, save the old one and put it somewhere where you won't lose it. Find a meadow and collect small bouquets of wildflowers. Lay them flat in different parts of the phone book. Place a small boulder, or anything else that's heavy and not likely to take off, on top of the phone book. Let sit for a few months.

Remove the flowers and place them in a pattern you like on the front of blank cards or on stiff artists' paper you can get at a craft or variety store. Attach them to the paper with a dab of glue. Peel an appropriate amount of transparent, self-stick plastic film (like Contact paper) from the roll and carefully place on top of the flowers, pressing from the center to the edge to eliminate air bubbles. Trim the edge of the plastic to match the card or paper. You can then send them to your friends for

69

Garden and the Great Outdoors

Christmas, birthdays, Valentine's Day or no reason at all. Bookmarks can be made in exactly the same way—just cut the paper to an appropriate size.

Mother Moon

I was in Arizona for a retreat at a time when the moon was waxing. We were doing a healing for a woman, and I suggested that she visualize herself as a small child and the moon as a dish, and that she climb in and curl up in it. She did so and found the experience immensely comforting. And that night I felt myself there too, as if I was in bright cave, absorbing all that bright reflected light.

Some people use mountains or trees as landmarks, but my reference point is the moon. I'm always aware of its cycles, and when I'm planning a journey or a time of creative work, I'll try to time it to coincide with the waxing moon. When the moon is new, like a bright thumbnail in the sky, it's full of the promise of growth, and it nourishes my growth as well.

The moon is like a mother to me. It has the energy and symbolism of a mother. What I can't get from a mother I get from the moon. I love the moon and the moon loves me.

> *"Peacefully the moon pauses over the rooftops,*
> *And hovers by the orchards,*

Lighting each distant mountain
In a picture of calm."

—Giacomo Leoparldi

Homemade Herbal Teas

It's easy to grow and make your own herbal teas, according to the folks at Yamagami's Nursery in Cupertino, California, who write that one way to start is to grow lemon verbena, lemon grass, spearmint, and peppermint. Lemon verbena is easy to grow in full sun to part shade. Prune frequently to keep it bushy. Widely used in Asian cuisine, lemon grass is a very fragrant clump grass that grows two to three inches tall. It likes full sun. Spearmint and peppermint like moist semi-shady areas; prune frequently to keep low and beware—they can be invasive so you might want to grow these two in containers.

You can throw a small handful of any or all of these fresh herbs into black tea before steeping—just be sure to wash them well beforehand. Or you can dry them and experiment with a variety of combinations and additions, including carefully washed rose petals and hips, chamomile buds or leaves, or lemon or orange slices. A good basic caffeine-free recipe is 3 tablespoons dried lemon verbena, 4 tablespoons dried lemon grass, 1 tablespoon dried spearmint, and 1 tablespoon dried peppermint. Simply crumble dried herbs together, steep in four

71

Garden and the
Great Outdoors

cups of boiling water for 5 minutes and strain. Delicious either
hot or iced.

A Four-Star Meal in a Stale Sandwich

One of the great pleasures of backpacking is how good the most
ordinary food tastes after a long day's hike from your base camp. You
come back exhausted to the home you've created in the woods, and
a handful of trail mix and a stale old sandwich becomes a four-star
meal, to be savored slowly while you watch the stars come out and
the bats flicker across the sky among the trees. If you have any energy left, you collect twigs and pieces of bark and shape the fire, light
it, nurse it, pile rocks around to reflect the heat, and boil water for
Kraft macaroni and cheese and a mug of hot chocolate.

Once the fire is going, there's the pleasure of laying your aching
body against the dirt, your back against an old log, waiting for the
water to boil in the blackened, beat-up tin pot while conversation
among old and trusted friends drifts through the darkness and settles
around the silences while you watch the sparks fly up. All the while,
you're thinking fondly of your sleeping bag and how you'll sleep so
deliciously deeply the moment you climb into it.

*"Cooking is at once one of the simplest and most gratify-
ing of the arts, but to cook well, one must love and respect
food."*

—Craig Claiborne

THINGS TO DO

Mom's Secret in Your Pocket

73

*Garden and the
Great Outdoors*

When a Brooklyn boy was grown up enough to move into a place of his own, he asked his mother for one of her cooking secrets. "How do you make your chocolate chip cookies?" "It's right off the package," she replied. "I mean, your recipe." "It's off the package. You can make them yourself."

And so he did, with some variations over the years for adult tastes. But, basically, there's no need to stray far from the instructions on the bag of chocolate chips to make this portable, fits-any-pocket-or-purse recollection of Mom's kitchen.

(Christopher Kimball, editor and publisher of *Cook's Illustrated* magazine, did an exhaustive series of tests—hey, it's a living—in search of the perfect chocolate chip cookie. Beginning with the standard recipe, he increased dark brown sugar and cut back on white sugar, substituted shortening for a portion of the butter, increased flour to 2-½ cups and used baking powder instead of baking soda. (There's no reason you, too, can't enjoy fiddling with it.) Be sure to pack some on your next camping trip.

Chocolate Chip Cookies

1 cup (2 sticks) butter, softened slightly

1 cup brown sugar

½ cup granulated sugar

2 eggs

2 teaspoons vanilla

2¼ cups all-purpose flour

1 teaspoon baking soda

1 teaspoon salt

12 ounces chocolate chips

1½ cups walnuts or pecans, broken or chopped

Cream butter until soft, add sugar, and cream until light and fluffy. Beat in eggs and vanilla.

Sift flour with baking soda and salt. Stir into creamed mixture, beating well. Stir in chocolate chips and nuts.

Drop by rounded tablespoons about 1½ inches apart on greased cookie sheets. Bake in 375-degree oven 9–12 minutes. Remove from pan immediately. Makes about 5 dozen cookies.

Country Pleasures

It would be wonderful if we all had friends with a country house who would invite us to spend the weekend when summer is oppressive in the city. You know—Adirondack chairs, fresh strawberries, and a colorful crowd that could entertain you like a cartoon in *The New Yorker* or a Noel Coward play.

But I've been more satisfied by simpler pleasures—just an afternoon in the country, thank you. The advantages are many: You can sleep in your own bed, not on a cot that's been on the porch for three seasons. You don't have to wait in line for a rusty stall shower. And, if you are visiting friends rather than picnicking in a field—after you've been your charming self for several hours—and you've enjoyed everybody's company, you can be home before dark. You can leave those mosquitoes in the country where they belong.

It's also easier to come up with an afternoon invitation. I offer to help fix lunch, pack the picnic basket, skim the leaves off the pool. I bring wine, fresh bread, those strawberries. You can do the same. Don't forget fresh flowers—your hosts are probably tired of those artfully arranged tomatoes and squash as a dining table centerpiece. If you're driving, nothing would be more welcome than an insulated chest filled with bags of ice cubes. And once you've helped clean up and relaxed through the afternoon, maybe you'll be invited back the next weekend. If not, simply take your picnic and find a spreading tree.

> *"Some people like to make a little garden out of life and walk down a path."*
>
> —Jean Anouilh

75

Garden and the Great Outdoors

Chess Above the Waterfall

When I was recovering from pneumonia in Dharamsala, I noticed people playing chess in cafés. I started playing at a little café near the top of a waterfall. The courtyard was surrounded by pieces of local slate covered with designs painted by travelers. The chess players would sit on stones in the sun, whiling away the morning and afternoon with tea brewed with milk and spices.

It was an odd group that included Russian expatriates, travelers from South America, an old bearded sea captain, and a rabid young Objectivist for whom winning was everything. I played them all, and sometimes I simply sat and watched the ebb and flow of play and the shifting combinations unfolding on different boards. What I remember most is the intense pleasure of concentrating all my cunning on a game that meant everything while it lasted and after it ended meant nothing, to either loser or winner. For there was always another game and more tea and the sun on the stones and the delicious feeling of being removed from time.

THINGS TO DO

Vacation Tips for Houseplants

While you are away from home, you can make sure that your plants don't end up in the great compost pile in the sky by following these simple tips:

- Before you leave, pull your plants out of hot spots so they will not dry out so quickly, and move them to the coolest, darkest spots in your house. Bring any deck plants inside, again to the coolest, darkest locations.

- Do not leave plants in a bucket of water or deep saucer while you are gone. Too much water can rot the roots. Instead, fill trays or saucers with pebbles and water and group plants together to raise humidity, and remember if the house is closed and lights are off, your plants will need less water.

- If you are going to be gone for any length of time, be sure to have someone come in and water once a week.

77

Garden and the Great Outdoors

Fleeting Pleasures

Instants of pleasure stolen between other instants, so that you know they must end quickly, have a special intensity. I remember being in Yosemite Park one morning after having breakfast, and the sun had just risen above the trees and was warming the rocks. And I remember the pleasure of the warm sun working its way into the cold morning and into my bones as I sat on the rock and knowing that I would soon be called to wash the camping dishes. The knowledge that I would have to leave this spot of trees and rocks and sun in a short minute made me feel pleasure and nostalgia bound up together in a way that was almost unbearable.

"In stillness there is fullness; in fullness there is nothing-
ness; in nothingness there are all things."

—Quaker saying

Outdoor Showers

One of the greatest things my mother ever did when we kids
were little was to introduce us to outdoor showers. It would be a hot
sticky summer day in New England, and suddenly a rainstorm would
come up. She would dress us in our bathing suits and let us run outside. The best part was standing under the drain spout and letting
the water beat down on our heads. The sense of freedom and excitement from doing something new, the relief from the heat and humidity, the peculiar smell of water meeting superheated asphalt—I can
still remember it forty years later.

"Talk of mysteries! Think of our life in nature—daily to
be shown matter, to come into contact with it—rocks,
trees, wind on our cheeks! The solid earth! The actual
world!"

—Henry David Thoreau

Lady in the Lake

I love to swim to music when I'm alone at the lake. I put on a special tape moments before a soulful trumpet solo. Then I run down to the dock, ditch my clothes, and get into the water. I move just enough to stay afloat without any sound, and I feel the water like warm brown silk on my body as the solo fills the air and drifts into the cedars that surround the lake. The combination of the music, the water, and the cheeky pleasure of wearing nothing but hummingbird earrings and pink nail polish gives me such profound comfort that the memory of it sustains me in the depth of winter.

> *"In the end, what affects your life most deeply are things too simple to talk about."*
>
> —Nell Blaine

79

Garden and the
Great Outdoors

THINGS TO DO

Toast the Birds

Next time you empty your toaster tray of crumbs, instead of throwing them in the trash, sprinkle them outside your kitchen window. You and the birds both will be treated.

Imagining Freedom

When I was a child in Sarawak, Malaysia, it was one of my jobs to climb trees and collect the fruit. This was a task I always looked forward to, because once I was up there I could see far out over the forest. I'd spend hours at the top of the tree, lost in fantasies as I stared into the distance. My flights of imagination took me far over the horizon, because I knew that beyond it were countries where the people weren't oppressed by their governments. I imagined what it would be like to be free, and all the things I'd do. My fantasies gave me hope and courage throughout my childhood.

"If we sincerely want harmony, peace and joy in our lives, we can have them, but we must be willing to do the work. We must make maintaining an awareness of our spiritual natures first in our lives. Our inner world is the architect of our external world. We don't lose faith in the goodness of life because we become angry and depressed. We become angry and depressed because we lose faith in the goodness of life."

—Susan L. Taylor

For Love of Weeds

I have a confession to make that I hope my father never hears—

I love weeding. During the summers when I was small, my father used to pay me fifty cents an hour to pull weeds from our extensive gardens. I suppose, looking back on my wage scale, it was a great deal for him, but it was even better for me. It was such a feeling of accomplishment to finish a square area and look down at all that sweet-smelling moist dirt and not see a single little invader.

Blessed with more garden space than one boy could keep weed-free, it seemed at the time a source of unlimited riches—all for doing what was fun in the first place. One particularly ambitious summer, I would set my alarm clock for sunrise in order to give myself time to weed away the morning hours and still leave plenty of time for more normal summer activities. At the tender age of ten, I planted a vegetable garden that covered nearly a quarter acre of land and worked diligently every day, weeding and playing Panama Canal with my extensive series of irrigation ditches.

All that training has conditioned me so strongly that now all I need to do to return to childlike peace is to plant myself in the garden. It must sound truly corny, but what a great way to get grounded—on your hands and knees in the dirt, face down, all attention focused on seeking out those unwanted little weeds.

> *"It gives one a sudden start in going down a barren,*
> *stony street, to see upon a narrow strip of grass, just*
> *within the iron fence, the radiant dandelion, shining in*
> *the grass, like a spark dropped from the sun."*
>
> —Henry Ward Beecher

81

Garden and the
Great Outdoors

Instant Gourmet

Make your own garlic-flavored olive oil, preferably from your very own garlic crop. Simply peel five cloves of garlic, add them to five cups of olive oil, cap the bottle and let it stand in a cool place for a week. This is a great way to recycle a pretty wine bottle and makes a fabulous gift.

Peppy Poppies

To prolong the life of poppies and other sap-filled flowers such as hibiscus, hollyhocks, clematis, and hellebores, try this trick before you arrange them. Cut the stems to the desired length then hold them over a match flame for a few seconds to sear the stems. This will seal the stems and keep the sap from draining out, extending the life of your bouquet.

Body and Soul

"When the well is dry, we know the worth of water."

—Benjamin Franklin

Body and Soul

Out on the Outrigger

Once when I was doing research in the Philippines, I was on a pump boat ferrying a group of scientists between two distant islands. As the boat moved through the swells, I lay on a plank lashed to the bamboo outrigger, trailing my hand through the ocean. The sound of the engine was soothingly hypnotic, as the outrigger skimmed through the swells. The feeling of being suspended and transported and cradled, as the sun caressed me and the water as warm as my body lapped at my skin, left me completely relaxed and aware of being relaxed. All my usual worries suddenly seemed quite unimportant. I felt as if I was physically shedding them. It's moments like these, when you're totally relaxed without putting any effort into it, that you're most likely to have life-changing insights. Today, when I feel the need to get a new perspective on my day-to-day concerns, I often think of that experience and how important it is for me to create the conditions where I can simply let go.

Relaxation Techniques

84

The following has been recommended in every publication from *Reader's Digest* to New Age healing manuals, but this step-by-step relaxation exercise really can relieve stress and tension.

Lie down on your back with your arms at your sides or lightly resting on your chest. If that's not possible, sit in a comfortable chair. Put your feet up if you can. Close your eyes. Take several deep breaths.

Relax your feet—you may want to say to yourself, "I am relaxing my feet. They are becoming more and more relaxed." Then go up your body, piece by piece doing the same thing to relax your ankles, legs, hips, buttocks, stomach, back, and shoulders. Follow through to your hands, arms, jaw, cheeks, eyes, forehead, and scalp.

Feel your entire body relax, and remain this way for five minutes. For a deeper state of relaxation, imagine yourself on an elevator, going from the tenth floor of a building to the first floor. Count the floors and relax at each one, as you did throughout your body.

There's another technique for relieving specific tension—particularly in the neck and shoulders—while you're working. Breathe deeply from your abdomen. Each time you exhale, imagine you are sending that healing breath to the part of your body that is sore or fatigued. If you do this for even one or two minutes, it will help.

The Open Road

85

Body and Soul

I guess I am a real Californian because one of the greatest pleasures in my life is driving. I have easily logged over a million miles in my car—all for pleasure. I don't like just any kind of driving—certainly not stop-and-go city driving—but long distance, open-road, trance-inducing driving. I stumbled on the therapeutic benefits of the lonesome highway when I was young and foolish. When things would get to the point where I couldn't deal with them anymore, I would jump in the car, make my way to the least traveled road around, and drive for hours.

Once, after I decided to drop out of college because everything in my life seemed to be going wrong, I took off into the Pacific Northwest where, driving on nothing but back roads and deserted logging tracks, I spent almost six weeks in constant motion. It about wrecked my 1962 Ford Fairlane, but it did wonders for my peace of mind.

It's hard for me to explain why it works so well. It's the physical sensation of the car vibrating down the road—the adult version of getting crying babies to go to sleep by putting them in a moving car. It's also the nonstop but ever-changing visual montage. And it's the sound—not sharp or distinct, but a low background hum. All together, they create a cocoon of safety where the dissociation between my body, which must remain focused and in control of the car, and my mind, which is freed to float aimlessly, can take place.

Icy Sheets

I grew up in a part of the South where it was often so hot and muggy on summer nights that my sisters and I couldn't get to sleep. Finally my parents came up with a solution to the problem. They told us we could each put one sheet in the fridge at supper. By bedtime the sheet would be crisp and cold, and when I crawled under it, the cool cotton draped over my skin was utterly calming. First I'd lie on the left side, and when that part of the sheet warmed up, I'd simply slide over one body width to where it was still cool. The sheet was exactly four body widths wide, but I was usually asleep before I used them all up. It felt so good I got to looking forward to going to bed, and sticky summer nights became a pleasure instead of an irritation.

THINGS TO DO

Cool and Soothing

When the weather is hot and sticky, refrigerate your facial toner, freshener, astringent or after-shave lotion. It will be as cool as the advertisements in the glossy magazines promise.

Here's another hot weather tip from the character Marilyn Monroe played in the movie version of *The Seven Year Itch*, George Axelrod's Broadway comedy. She chilled her underwear in the refrigerator before getting dressed.

87

Body and Soul

Jalapeño Peppers

My mother told me that the first solid food I ate in my high chair was jalapeño peppers. That was in Texas. I've lived many different places since then, but I can hardly recall a day when I didn't have jalapeño peppers. The older I grow, the hotter I like them. Whenever I go out to a restaurant, I stick a jalapeño in my purse so I'll have one to munch on if the meal isn't hot enough. I read somewhere recently that jalapeño peppers contain a natural antidepressant. I guess that's why I always feel so high.

Jalapeños Con Crema

A little jalapeño pepper can go a long way. Here's one way to extend their bite in a rich but peppery cornbread.

Jalapeno Cornbread

2 eggs, lightly beaten

¼ cup vegetable oil

2 jalapeño peppers, finely chopped

½ cup sour cream

1 cup (1 small can) creamed corn

1½ cups yellow cornmeal

2 teaspoons baking powder

½ teaspoon salt

1 cup grated cheddar cheese

Preheat oven to 350 degrees. Grease a 9-inch cast iron skillet or other heavy pan.

Mix eggs, oil, peppers, sour cream, and corn in a medium bowl. Thoroughly mix cornmeal, baking powder, and salt in a large bowl, then quickly stir in liquid ingredients. Batter may be slightly lumpy. Pour half the batter into pan. Sprinkle with cheese. Cover with remaining batter.

Bake 25-30 minutes until wooden pick inserted in center comes out clean. Cool at least 10 minutes before turning out of pan, or slice in pan and serve. Makes 6 servings.

Ice-Cream Floats

One of the great advantages of adulthood is being able to have ice-cream floats whenever I feel like it. It also means I can test the float rules that I stood by when I was a child. I'm an ice-cream-first person. I have friends who swear you have to put the ice cream after the pop so it won't fizz. I know for sure that fizz is better, and the straw is the perfect device for sweeping the fizz around the glass. This is an important element of the float-drinking ritual. My technique for actually eating the float is to plunge the straw through the center and suck with might and main to draw the ice cream and pop up together in the same mouthful. Pussyfooting around with dinky spoons is not the way to get the most pleasure out of a ice-cream float.

Choice of pop is important. I remember one time when I had a really stressful day, I went to the convenience store and got Seven-Up. This satisfied my need to deviate from tradition and test my boundaries, but I wouldn't do it again. Pop for a float needs a vibrant color to contrast with the vanilla ice cream. Brown or gray doesn't cut it. My friends can do what they want, but I've been an Orange Crush woman for thirty years, and I'm sticking to it.

89

Body and Soul

> *"I doubt the world holds for anyone a more soul-stirring surprise than the first adventure with ice cream."*
>
> —Heywood Broun

THINGS TO DO

When the French novelist Stendhal first tasted ice cream, he declared, "What a pity this isn't a sin!" You may judge for yourself.

Homemade Vanilla Ice Cream

3 cups half-and-half

¾ cup sugar

6 egg yolks

2 teaspoons vanilla extract

In a heavy saucepan, bring the half-and-half just to the simmering point over medium heat.

In a heatproof bowl, whisk together the sugar and egg yolks until well blended. Gradually pour the hot half-and-half into the egg mixture, whisking continually.

Return mixture to saucepan and cook over medium-low heat, stirring with a wooden spoon, until the custard is thick enough to coat a spoon, about 5 minutes.

Pour the custard through a strainer into a clean bowl and refrigerate until cold. Transfer the custard to an ice cream freezer and follow manufacturer's instructions for freezing. If possible, let stand 2 or 3 hours before serving. Makes about 5 cups.

Touching the Earth

If I were about to die and I could no longer move or walk about, I'd want a bucket of earth beside my bed. The earth would be familiar, for it would come from my garden, where I'm intimate with the smell and the feel of the soil. Summer after summer, I've buried my hands in the ground and felt its warmth on my fingers as I've nudged weeds from its grasp. When I'm coming to terms with the end of my life, I want to be able to touch the soil that has given life to so many memories that I hold dear.

> *"Talking of Pleasure, this moment I was writing with one hand and with the other holding to my Mouth a Nectarine—good God how fine. It went down soft, pulpy, slushy, oozy—all its delicious embodiment melted down my throat like a large Beautiful strawberry."*
>
> —John Keats

91

Body and Soul

Buying a Ticket

Whether it's for a trip, a performance or a lottery, buying a ticket is a first step towards commitment to a journey, either physical or imaginary. It's the procurement of a passport, a decision to enter. It's

an act that creates or defines possibilities and choices. It's the door
to the avenue of delightful anticipation.

Seashells

Recently I dreamed about the Leonardo da Vinci drawing that
illustrates perfect proportion: the nude man facing forward, his arms
and legs outstretched to touch the circumference of a circle. But at
his crotch, my man had a glowing shell. Even in my dream I laughed.
Every room I live in has a shell or a picture of one in it. This started
when I was small. My godmother, one of those wandering women
who find adventure and fulfillment in widowhood, used to send me
postcards of seashells from Florida, where she spent her winters. She
wrote to me about coastal islands where shells covered the beaches,
and if you dived down deep enough, the ocean floor too. I longed to
see those beaches and swim in those warm seas.

I moved from pictures to the real things. I found my first shell,
a pink and white one that I still have, at the local fishmarket. No two
shells are ever exactly alike. Their shapes and patterns are as beautiful and diverse as snowflakes. Shells' nature is mysterious: They are
skeletons worn outside soft flesh, bones that come in the color of
warm skin—pinks, whites, creams, browns, blacks. (Blues and
greens, the colors of cold and ice, are rare in shells from warm seas.)
Most shell colors don't become me, but I like keeping shells around

me. The idea of a shield worn on your back, a pretty one, perhaps pearlescent, that protects you no matter where you go, has always appealed to me. As a teenager, when I felt most like a tender mollusc, I made myself pale green curtains covered with a shell print. Lying in bed, I could imagine myself underwater, perfectly safe.

A Personal Pick-Me-Up

93

Body and Soul

To evoke the simplicity of gentler times, do as nineteenth century women did, make yourself a fresh herbal or floral water. You can use these delightfully fragranced waters in many ways. Use them as you would a body splash or toilet water, place them in a bowl to scent your home, or put them in an atomizer and use them to infuse your home or body with sweet fragrance.

Basic Recipe for Herbal or Floral Waters

3 cups of distilled water

¼ cup of vodka (unlike rubbing alcohols, vodka will not add its own scent to the mixture)

1 ounce dried flowers, or 8 to 10 drops of essential oil (this is a guide only, use more or less to your own taste)

Measure the water into a bottle, add the vodka, then mix in the flowers, herbs, or oils. Let the mixture stand, covered, in a dark, cool place for seven days. You can leave the herbs or flowers in if you want, or if they aren't as attractive as when you started (this is often the case) simply strain them out.

Anonymous in New York

The thing I love about New York is you have to work really hard to look weird enough for people to notice you. Anywhere outside of Midtown, so many people look so bizarre that they'll see you if you look weird, but you won't make a splash. You can sing in the street, shout poetry—whatever. You're absolutely free to be whoever you are.

This is the best kind of freedom for slobs like me. Now I live in the country, and when I go to the store in my studio clothes, they look so disreputable that everyone stares at me. I get a real kick out of going back to New York and being totally anonymous.

"Beware all enterprises that require new clothes."

—Henry David Thoreau

Playing with Hair

I have always liked it when someone plays with my hair. Once, when I worked in a remote village on Baffin Island in the Arctic, I didn't know anyone to begin with and no one touched me for ages. Then one day I went clam-digging with an Inuit woman who was beginning to become a friend. We stayed the night in a Boy Scout hut down the coast, and in the evening her daughters, fascinated with my strange blonde hair, played with it for hours, combing it, braiding it, pulling it. I wanted them to never stop.

95

Body and Soul

THINGS TO DO

Our informal survey has uncovered that many people love their hair played with, and even more love their heads rubbed. Giving a wonderful head massage is not at all difficult. Here's how: Stand behind the person and place your hands very gently on her head and just rest there for a few seconds; the idea is to have the two of you relax and for you to get in tune with her. If it is comfortable for her, have her close her eyes. Place both hands on top of her head, so they meet at the midline. Using all your fingers of both hands, press and massage in circular motions, covering the entire scalp from forehead to nape of neck, and from ear to ear. Ask the recipient to guide you as to how much pressure. Pay particular attention—use your thumbs—to where the base of the skull meets the neck.

Massage her temples in a firm, circular motion for a minute or so. Then slowly massage your way across the forehead until your hands meet in the middle. Return to the temples and then bring your hands down either side of her head to the point in from of the earlobes where you can feel a bulge when she clenches her jaw. Massage there. Finally, finish off with the Hair Pull. Gently grab a hunk of hair with each hand and tug upwards very gently for a few seconds. Then grab another hunk and repeat, moving on through the entire head. (You can also do this to yourself, which is very nice, but not quite as pleasurable.)

For an altogether different head rush, be daring and massage your favorite essential oil directly onto your hair (after you've tested it on a small patch on your arm to be sure you aren't allergic). You'll walk in a cloud of your favorite scent all day! To find just the right fragrance for you, make a trip to places like Body Time, The Body Shop, or Bare Escentuals, and sniff the samples till you find just the perfect one.

Friends and Family

*"Own only what you can always carry with you:
Know languages, know countries, know people. Let your
memory be your travel bag."*

—Alexander
Solzhenitsyn

Conversation for Its Own Sake

For the past ten years, I have been selling handmade art at Seattle's Pike Place Market. When business is slow, I indulge myself in the simple pleasure of conversation for conversation's sake. I meet people from all over the country, and all over the world, and routinely ask them where they are from. Part of this is practical—I need to know if customers are local in order to know how much background information to provide about my Northwest Coast style jewelry and the petroglyph rubbings I sell. But I am genuinely interested in people and places, and since I cannot go to other parts of the world, I let the world come to me.

I can often surprise people by guessing where they come from, usually from a distinctive accent, but also from other clues, primarily sartorial. And once I know where they're from, the conversation just naturally takes off. If I mention to an Irish visitor that my grandfather was born in County Tyrone, I might receive in return a string of anecdotes about Irish life. From Palestinians I have received recommendations on books to read on the history of Palestine. With Norwegians, I am quick to mention my relations in their country, and perhaps try out the little Norwegian I know.

And so the days pass. Every morning I set up my display; every evening I break down and roll back across the bricks to my locker, sometimes richer in dollars, but almost always richer in experience. I was particularly flattered to have a friend from the Louisiana Delta country comment to me that I was the only non-Southerner he had met who indulged in conversation as a pastime, for its own sake. And I thought I just liked to talk and listen.

Treehouses

When I was growing up, I used to spend a lot of time in a treehouse in a field behind our house. This was southern Illinois, so the countryside was flat, and when I was up there I could see across the whole town. There was a little platform with just enough room for a couple of people, and it was a perfect place for inviting special friends and excluding the kids I didn't like. This was around the time

I was getting crushes on guys, and I'd sit up there and fantasize that Kevin O'Sullivan would come up and visit me.

Later, when I went to college in Ohio, my friends and I came across another treehouse in a little forest near the railroad trestle. We called it "the Secret Laughing Place," because it had obviously been built by some kids and we imagined the fun they must have had there. It soon became our secret laughing place too, this treehouse where we'd go to share our hopes and fears and dreams.

> *"That is the best—to laugh with someone because you both think the same things are funny."*
>
> —Gloria Vanderbilt

99

Friends and Family

A Child's Confidant

When our son was about eight, we sent him away to camp and he came back so distressed that he was afraid to go to bed with the light out. He couldn't tell me what had happened; he could only show me how he felt. When I was trying to figure out what to do, I started thinking about Curious George. I used to read that book to him at bedtime, and he loved it so much—I must have read it a hundred times. A few days later I went to a toy store and bought a monkey that looked a lot like Curious George. He was a puppet with arms and legs that had velcro strips so that he would cling on to your arms if you were a grownup or around your waist if you were a little child.

My son took to the puppet instantly and named him George. He told George all about his troubles, and the three of us would have wonderful conversations. A short time later he seemed a lot happier and stopped being afraid of the dark. After that the two of them were inseparable. My son used to suck his thumb and rub the fringe of an old frayed blanket against his nose. It just so happened that George had a white tuft of fur on his forehead, and my son would velcro George onto his body and rub that fringe of fur against his nose every night when he went to sleep.

Years later, when my son got a scholarship to a hockey school a thousand miles from home, he left George behind, and I was secretly glad because now it was my turn to be comforted by George. Whenever I felt really sad about my son's being gone, I'd walk around the house all day, doing whatever I had to do, with George locked onto my arm. I'd talk to him like an old friend who knew both me and my son and could therefore understand my distress, and I always felt so much better after I told him my troubles.

The Temple Cloth Printers

There's a street in India where a family of temple cloth printers works under a makeshift shelter. I visited them several years ago, and when I left I promised to come back and see them. Of course they didn't believe me—it's what every traveler says when they make a special connection with someone and then disappear from their lives.

Four years later I returned to India, and I went back to see them. It took a moment for them to recognize me and me them. Their kids had grown up and were completely different from the children I remembered, just as my child was different from the child they had met. We all cried. It's like a small miracle when you make the commitment to return to someone. The connection becomes deeper, layered with remembered experience.

101

Friends and Family

Teenage Epiphanies

My son called me from his sailing camp the other day and said, "Dad, can't we go sailing instead of biking for our holidays?" I had to refrain from saying, "I told you so." You wouldn't believe the fight he'd put up to get out of taking sailing courses. It's a big payoff when kids finally realize the value of some activity you've sweated blood to get them to appreciate. It made my day when I came back from a hiking trip with my other son and he muttered, "That wasn't too bad." In teenage language that means "I had a great time." If I'd told him a year earlier he might have fun just walking in the mountains he'd have given me that look that means, "Dad, I know you mean well, but you're totally nuts."

"Everything I did in my life that was worthwhile I caught Hell for."

—Earl Warren, chief
justice of the United
States

One Hundred Eighty Seconds of Happiness

102

The joy, when nursing an infant, of feeling the little, soft, warm, almost moist hands butterflying on one's breast, and knowing that right then to that one human being one is essential—that is happiness.

One of my heroes, a Swedish writer named Gunnar Ekelof (whom, if he had written in a major language, we would all study in school), writes that every human being is allowed 180 seconds of pure and unmitigated happiness—not 180 seconds at once, but 180 seconds total in our lives.

If he's right I have gotten more than my share. With each of my children I have experienced more than 180 seconds of the pure happiness where every instinct, every reason, every rational thought and every irrational emotion work together in a glorious whole.

"The soul should always stand ajar, ready to welcome the ecstatic experience."

—Emily Dickinson

The Long and Winding Trail

The first couple of hours on a really long hike can be awkward and painful, but then a rhythm develops as my body relaxes, and I begin to feel like I could do this all day long and never get tired. Through years of use, my leather boots have taken on the shape of my feet. They're soft but substantial, and I love the feel of their weight on my feet as my legs move like pendulums along the forest trail with no feeling of effort at all.

Throughout the day, the changing light transforms the appearance of shrubs and trees like a slow-moving film. And always there is the music and the beauty of the birds—warblers bright as limes, the tangerine flash of Baltimore orioles, the glimpse of a redtail hawk gliding far above the canopy of trees. And the passing fragrance of a cottonwood bursting into leaf, if it's spring, or the occasional punky scent of bear. And everywhere the soft enveloping drone of bees. And the sweet taste of blueberries I snatch from a bush without breaking stride. And in this place at this time I feel perfectly at home in my skin with all my senses in ecstasy and my mind empty of care and my heart delighting to be in the company of friends who are enjoying this day every bit as much as I.

103

Friends and Family

> *"I always held that the great high privilege, relief and comfort of friendship was that one had to explain nothing."*
>
> —Katherine Mansfield

A Old-Fashioned Taffy Pull

My mother is one of those hardy New Englanders who believes in thriftiness, simplicity, and tradition. So when we were growing up, we always made handmade birthday cards (why buy them when you can make them?) and got books from the library (why buy them when you can borrow them?). She was the mother teaching all the kids in the neighborhood how to make snowmen, and organizing the neighborhood annual Christmas carol sing or croquet tournament; if it was about having fun for free (or almost), she was in charge. So of course the taffy pull was her idea. We jaded late twentieth century kids were skeptical, to say the least—wasn't taffy that horrible colored salt water stuff sold at beaches along the Eastern Seaboard and didn't making the stuff at home go out with high-topped shoes? "Oh pish," she said, "stop being party poopers," as she rounded up at least seven kids from down the street. "We're going to do it."

And do it we did—and yes it was fun, particularly with a crowd. Now that I am a parent and those values of my mother's seem to be right in vogue, I, too, encourage my kids to make their own cards and they—and all their friends—love to make taffy together. It's a lot of fun—all you need is a candy thermometer and some pairs of willing arms. But before you start, be sure to read the directions all the way through—it does require some expertise. And above all, don't leave the little ones alone—the hot syrup can be dangerous!

Vanilla Taffy

1¼ cups sugar

¼ cup water

2 tablespoons rice wine vinegar, or ordinary vinegar

1½ teaspoons butter

1 teaspoon vanilla

In a medium saucepan over low heat, stir together the sugar, water, vinegar, and butter until sugar is dissolved. Turn heat up to medium and cook, without stirring, until the syrup reaches 265 degrees as registered on a candy thermometer. Pour onto a buttered platter (be careful not to be splattered by the hot syrup—hold the pouring edge away from you and pour slowly) and let cool until a dent can be made in it when pressed with a finger. Sprinkle the vanilla on top and gather the taffy into a ball. Take care in picking up the mass; it could still be very hot in the center.

105

Friends and Family

Pull	Fold	Cut

When you can touch it, start pulling it with your hands to a length of about 18 inches. Then fold it back onto itself. Repeat this action until the taffy becomes a crystal ribbon. Then start twisting as well as folding and pulling. (See diagram on next page). Pull until the ridges begin to hold their shape. Depending on your skill, the weather and the cooking process, this can take from between 5 and 20 minutes. Roll into long strips and cut into 1-inch pieces. Makes ½ pound.

Bringing Out the Child

Parenting brings out the joyful kid in me. Last week we went to the lake to visit our son's friends. It was the kind of dull day when adults stay indoors, but the kids weren't having any of that. We ended up being towed in inner tubes behind a boat, and that inevitably led to a water fight. I wouldn't normally be found running around waving an AK-47 water gun, but the kids' enthusiasm was contagious. For a moment I forgot all about those injunctions and rules that keep grownups from acting silly.

The activities our children include us in are one of the greatest pleasures of parenting. More and more as they grow older, the things we enjoy are driven by their interests. For the last four months they've been intensely involved in baseball, and we've connected with a lot of people we wouldn't ordinarily meet. When our son's team went on to the finals and won the tournament, fifteen other parents came along to root with us. Having children has given us a sense of community in a way we never dreamed of before.

Beading Together

One great thing to do with kids is to buy an assortment of inexpensive beads (bead and craft stores abound these days) and host a beading party for a group. If you have very young children, you can use dry macaroni (instead of beads that can be popped into mouths) that they can decorate with paint or glitter. You can then help kids string them onto elastic for easy bracelets and necklaces. For older beaders, buy bead thread, beading needles, and clasps to finish off their creations.

107

Friends and Family

Brief Pleasures

Getting the giggles someplace where it is completely inappropriate, like the library, but only if your friend does, too.

Putting on a warm flannelette nightie fresh out of the dryer.

The soft furry stems of tomato plants in August, and the pungent fragrance of their leaves.

Freezing chocolate chip cookies before they're completely cooked, then dipping them into hot tea.

Hearing a friend put into words an unformed thought of your own that you wanted to express but couldn't.

Planting flowers in someone else's garden that they won't find out about till the spring.

Going back to sleep after breakfast in bed.

The first bite of sushi.

Taking a nap on Sunday afternoon with the smell of roast beef in the air and the distant sound of pots and pans meaning that someone else is doing the cooking.

The moment when a good book reaches its turning point and
you feel the threads coming together into a new under-
standing and catharsis.

A long, slow kiss, and the feel of soft lips against my mouth and
gentle, loving hands on my body.

The peace and quiet of Christmas night after everyone else has
gone to bed and all the commotion is over.

Finding the warm spot in the bed where the hot water bottle
was before you moved it with your feet.

Walking at dusk on a city street and glimpsing moments of lives
unfolding in windows.

Standing on a sandy ocean beach facing the shore while the
water from the surf runs out and I feel like I'm traveling
backwards fast while the sand disappears under my feet.

Fall

A bright autumn moon . . .
In the shadow of each grass
an insect chirping

—Buson

Home

"The world has become too full of many things, an overfurnished room."

—Freya Stark

Pendulum Clocks

The thing I remember best about my grandfather's house when I visited him as a child was the sound of his old-fashioned pendulum clocks—the fat marble library clock on the mantelpiece, the cuckoo clock on the kitchen wall, and the tall grandfather clock looming in the corner of the parlor. While my grandfather puttered around, I'd sit on the floor, watching the dust motes float through shafts of sun streaming into the room, listening to the three clocks tick-tocking at different speeds—the library clock and cuckoo clock quick and high-pitched, the grandfather clock ponderous and low. The rhythm was like a calming life force, and it made me feel utterly at peace while I waited for the music of the chimes to signal the hour.

"The test of pleasure is the memory it brings."

—Jean-Paul Richter

THINGS TO DO

Uncommon Scents

114

Aromatics and sachets can bring pleasure and emotional resonance to a home, and they don't require major investment. Aromatics can be set out in beautiful containers for parties or intimate gatherings. New York chef Matthew Kenney, who adapted Moroccan cuisine for his restaurant, fills bowls at home with a combination of fragrant star anise, cardamom pods, and cinnamon sticks.

Old-fashioned sachets, for linen closets or dresser drawers, can be made simply with mixtures of dried lavender flowers and cedar shavings (sold at hardware stores as a moth deterrent), or such fragrant blends as dried rose petals, eucalyptus, and dried citrus peel. Mix a blend of your liking and pack it loosely in squares of muslin, layers of cheesecloth, or lightweight handkerchiefs (you can find vintage ones in thrift stores). Tie them with ribbon. These make great housewarming gifts.

Neat Nails

When life gets chaotic and overwhelming and I feel the need to be alone, I go off to my workshop, put on '60s music and reorganize my tools and nails. Bringing order out of chaos in my workshop calms me down and makes me more able to create order in the rest of my life.

"Luxury need not have a price—comfort itself is a luxury."

—Geoffrey Beene

115

Home

THINGS TO DO

Help with Clutter

When we asked people about their simple pleasures, we were surprised to discover how many people had, at the top of their list, straightening up their environment in some way. We received many stories of the satisfactions of a clean desk, the joy of reorganizing all the clothes in the closet, the thrill of throwing away unneeded possessions. For those who might want some help in experiencing such pleasures, we offer as good resources: *Organizing for the Creative Person*, by Dorothy

Lehmkuhl and Dolores Cotter Lamping, *Best Organizing Tips* and *How to Get Organized When You Don't Have the Time* by Stephanie Winston, and *Simply Organized* by Cris Evatt.

Sacred Soup

Ritual is important when I'm making soup. It begins with standing in my bare feet on the cool tile floor of my kitchen. I'm alone with lots of space around me and sacred cathedral music filling the air. I always chop the vegetables in the same order—onions and celery first—and I always chop the ends off first and then cut the vegetables in half. Each vegetable has its own smell and shape and texture, and I take great pleasure in handling them.

The ritual is so familiar that all parts of me feel in harmony. The meditative pleasure is enhanced by the knowledge that what I'm doing will bring pleasure to my family as well, especially when the weather's bad or someone's sick and I'm responding to the needs of my husband or children.

> *"Food imaginatively and lovingly prepared, and eaten in good company, warms the being with something more than the mere intake of calories."*
>
> —Marjorie Kinnan Rawlings

A Frugal Feast

Is there any food more comforting than soup? For immigrants to North America, it has always offered a taste of the homeland and a meal that could be stretched to satisfy expanding families. It might be chicken soup from Eastern Europe or the Vietnamese Pho of shredded meat and vegetables in broth. For Italians, the common denominator was pasta and bean soup, pasta e fagioli. In her reminiscence with recipes, *We Called It Macaroni* (Alfred A. Knopf, 1996), Nancy Verde Barr recalls that "pasta fazool" didn't seem like much of a treat when she was growing up. But when she was pregnant with her first child, she began to crave this comforting soup, and made many a mad dash to Italian restaurants in Providence, Rhode Island, for a container of hot, soothing soup to go. Here's one version, although as with most comfort food, there are dozens of equally tasty variations.

117

Home

Pasta e Fagioli

1 cup dried white or cranberry beans, or 2½ cups canned beans, drained and rinsed

¼ pound bacon, chopped or 2 ounces pancetta, minced

2 tablespoons olive oil (if using pancetta)

1 onion, finely chopped

1 rib celery, finely chopped

1 carrot, peeled and finely chopped

2 cloves garlic, minced

2–4 tomatoes, peeled and chopped

salt and fresh ground pepper

¼ pound small, tubular macaroni or noodles

Parmesan or pecorino cheese

If using dried beans, soak overnight in water, drain, cover again with water and simmer for about 2 hours, or until beans are tender. Set aside.

In a large saucepan, fry bacon until barely crisp or saute pancetta in olive oil about 4 minutes, until fat is rendered. Drain off most of fat.

Add the onion, celery, carrot, and garlic, and saute gently about 10 minutes, until vegetables are soft.

If using canned beans, heat in 4 cups water or meat broth. If using dried beans, reheat in a large pot. Add bacon vegetable mixture and tomatoes to beans, return to a simmer, add macaroni or noodles and cook until pasta is tender. Serve warm with freshly ground pepper and grated Parmesan or pecorino cheese. Serves 6.

Satisfying Setups

All around my house I have little collections of objects that I put together for their prettiness or sentimental value. Some people call these altars, but I call them "setups"—areas of visual pleasure that my eye will fall upon so that I see order and beauty even when the rest of the room is in total chaos. Setups might be candles and flowers, or pebbles and shells I've been given by special friends or collected on a favorite beach, or the fimo animals my son made before he grew up and took to snowboarding. Setups may mean nothing to other people who come into the house, but to me they're a constant source of pleasure.

> *"'Mid pleasures and palaces though we may roam*
> *Be it ever so humble, there's no place like home."*
>
> —John Howard Payne

119

Home

THINGS TO DO

You can create an altar or other meaningful contemplative space in just about any nook or cranny of your house—a book shelf, a ledge above the bathtub, a small table in your bedroom. The point is to pick an empty place where you will be often, so that you can enjoy it. What you decide to place there is, of course, entirely up to you. But whatever you put there should be something you feel really compelled to place there. It should be for you, not to please your great-aunt Tilly who gave you that hideous green statue that you really wish some child would conveniently break.

Drinking Vessels

I firmly believe that the pleasure you get from a refreshing liq-uid—whether it's coffee, hot chocolate, or juice—depends as much on the vessel you drink from as it does on the drink itself. My coffee mug has to look pretty, and it has to be light while having enough substance that it won't break in my hand. The most important thing is how the rim feels on my lips. If it feels rough or thick, that mug is down for the count and won't get used.

I make a point of using my best fancy glasses for everyday events. I just pretend I'm a very special visitor at my own table. It's such a pleasure to have my morning juice in an elegant crystal stem glass instead of the old jam jar.

"We plan, we toil, we suffer—in the hope of what? A camel-load of idol's eyes? The title deeds to Radio City? The empire of Asia? A trip to the moon? No, no, no, no. Simply to wake up just in time to smell the coffee and bacon and eggs. And, again I cry, how rarely it hap-pens! But when it does happen—then what a moment, what a morning, what a delight!"

—J.B. Priestley

THINGS TO DO

If you are a hot chocolate lover, try spicing it up with peppermint. Either melt a couple peppermint candies by stirring them into the pot while you're making the hot chocolate (taste test to get the amount right), or serve the chocolate in mugs with a whole candy cane as a stirrer.

Sharpening Pencils

When I sharpen my colored pencils, the curls of color create a kaleidoscopic world that delights me. Regular pencils crumble, but with colored pencils the wooden part comes off in a swirl like ballerina skirts with brilliant fringes. Sharpening them is as much of a pleasure as coloring with them.

> *"One can get just as much exultation in losing oneself in a little thing as in a big thing. It is nice to think how one can be recklessly lost in a daisy!"*
>
> —Anne Morrow
> Lindbergh

121

Home

Potato Comfort

High on the list of universal comfort foods is potatoes. And when you are talking a real fall treat, there is nothing to compare to garlic and potatoes together. Is it possible that no one combined mashed potatoes and garlic before "garlic mashed potatoes" appeared on trendy restaurant menus and food magazine covers in the 1990s? We think not. The ancient bulb that the Chinese were praising in 3000 B.C. and the tuber that Spanish conquistadors discovered in Peru in the 16th century A.D. were surely meant for each other—two great underground resources merged into creamy bliss.

You can, if you like, simply toss peeled garlic cloves into the water when you boil potatoes and mash them together. But for a little more elegance, simmer the garlic in milk and cream while the potatoes cook. It will all come together perfectly.

Garlic Mashed Potatoes

1½ pounds russet (baking) potatoes

8–10 cloves garlic

½ cup milk

½ cup cream

4–6 tablespoons butter

Salt and freshly ground black pepper to taste

Peel the potatoes, cut in half if large, cover with salted water and boil until tender, about 20 minutes. Drain, return to pot and shake until water is evaporated.

Meanwhile, peel garlic and slice in half lengthwise. If there is a green sprout in the center of the clove, lift it out and discard. Place garlic cloves, milk and cream in a small saucepan. Bring to a boil and cook, at lowest possible simmer, until garlic is tender, about 20 minutes.

Remove the garlic with a fork or slotted spoon. Put the potatoes and garlic together through a ricer or food mill, if possible. Using an old-fashioned potato masher, mash potatoes and garlic together in a large bowl, adding butter, then milk and cream mixture, a little at a time, until desired consistency is reached. Add a little of the water in which the potatoes were boiled if needed.

Season with salt and pepper to taste. Serves 4.

123

Home

THINGS TO DO

Scented Notepaper

We all send letters so infrequently these days that when we do, it should be a pleasurable experience for both the sender and the receiver. You can add a romantic touch to your personal correspondence by scenting your stationery. It's incredibly easy. This makes enough for you and your friends.

8 ounces unscented talcum powder
15 drops of your favorite essential oil or perfume

6 small, closely woven, cotton or silk bags, open on one side
ribbon
notepaper and envelopes
1 plastic bag

In bowl, combine the powder and perfume. Cover tightly and let sit for a day. Spoon the mixture into the bags and tie with ribbon. Place the bags in between the layers of notepaper and envelopes in a box and put the box into the plastic bag. Allow to sit for a few days so that the scent will permeate the paper. Makes 6 sachets.

Garden and the Great Outdoors

"No occupation is so delightful to me as the culture of the earth . . . and no culture comparable to that of the garden . . . But though an old man, I am but a young gardener."

—Thomas Jefferson

Emma's Tree

Our daughter was born in August but didn't come home from the hospital till November. To celebrate, we planted a quince tree in her honor, with her name attached. Now Emma's Tree bears fruit every November, at the anniversary of her homecoming, and we all make quince jam together. It's a reminder to her and her parents of just how special she is.

Plants that are tributes to people add joy to any garden. A gardener I knew who died of AIDS bequeathed his beloved pots of sedums to a plant store to be auctioned off so others could get pleasure from them too. His friends came out in droves, and the bidding was fierce. And now there are sedum reminders of him in gardens everywhere.

Other friends of ours decided to plant a rose for each of their children. There are so many specialty roses, you can find one for just about any name. They found a rose called Molly and a rose called Harry, but when it came Solomon's turn, they couldn't find a rose with his name. It just so happened that Solomon loved Elvis Presley. Now, when the roses come into bloom, Solomon knows that Graceland is just for him.

"If I do nothing else in my lifetime but leave the world a good tree, I've done something."

—Ray Bracken,
nurseryman

The Bulb Gatherer

In the fall, I go out in the garden and dig in the dirt for treasure: clumps of bulbs that were only a single bulb in spring. I divide them up and find a new home for each bulb to start another family. Then I do my best to forget where I've put them so I can be pleasantly surprised in spring. If everyone did this conscientiously, the whole earth would eventually be covered in daffodils and tulips and hyacinths. Squirrels can't do it all by themselves. What the world needs now is a Johnny Tulipbulb.

"For all things produced in a garden, whether of salads or fruits, a poor man will eat better that has one of his own, than a rich man that has none."

—J.C. Loudon

Forcing Bulbs

127

*Garden and the
Great Outdoors*

You can send away for kits from fancy mail-order nurseries that will let you grow bulbs indoors before their normal blooming season. Or you can put together your own for little more than the cost of the bulbs.

The traditional choice is narcissus, which offers clusters of small, fragrant flowers. The ones called Paperwhites are almost foolproof for blossoms as early as Christmas, if you start them in the middle of November.

Begin with a shallow, waterproof pot or bowl. A glass one lets you watch the roots develop and keep track of the water level. But you can use almost any container—try big, inexpensive soup plates that you can place around the house. Buy enough bulbs to fill the pot one layer deep with the bulbs about a half inch apart. First spread a layer of pebbles, available from garden supply stores, to a level that reaches a few inches below the rim of the pot.

Place the bulbs on the pebbles with the flat end down, pointed end up. Fill the pot in with more pebbles to keep the bulbs upright. Fill the pot with water so it just reaches the bottom of the bulbs. If possible, move the pot to a cool, dark place, such as a basement or unheated garage. This will encourage the roots to grow first. But if you don't have a place to hide the bulbs away, they should grow just as well indoors.

In a few weeks, the leaves will be about 3 inches high. That's the time to move the pot to a warmer, brighter location. As the plants grow—you can almost see them inching upward—and flowers develop, add water, but only to the base of the bulbs. Don't let them drown. You'll be rewarded with a mass of showy blossoms that perfume a room for weeks.

128

A Country Road

There's a dirt road near my farm that I walk over and over, year after year, and though I think I'm thoroughly familiar with it, I'm constantly finding new details to enjoy. A different aspect of light or a change in the weather can transform ordinary objects into exotic sights. One day last fall, I came across a huge broadleaf maple that had dropped its leaves on the road. A heavy frost had formed tall crystals of ice, and in the low slanting light of morning the crisp mass of leaves lay like satin draped over a piano, with little skyscrapers of ice rising up among the folds. Walking that road is a never-ceasing adventure.

"There is a pleasure in the pathless woods,
There is a rapture on the lonely shore.
There is a society, where none intrudes,
By the deep sea, and music in its roar:
I love not man the less, but Nature more."

—Lord Byron

THINGS TO DO

Web Time

Take time on a damp October morning to observe a spider weave her web in the garden. Watch her as she moves inside the rim, patiently and methodically, reaching out her leg to catch a strand of silk from her own body, threading it to a spoke and moving on, repeating the motion again and again. It will make you marvel at the endless magic of nature. More importantly, 20 minutes in her company will fill you with calm.

Garden and the
Great Outdoors

The Woodpecker Tree

Sometimes when I'm walking in the woods, I'll hear a woodpecker hammering away in the distance. If I can figure out which tree it's on, I move towards it very quietly, so I don't scare the bird away. When I press my ear to the bark and close my eyes, the blows from the woodpecker's bill reverberate so loudly it feels like I'm right inside the tree. It's like being able to hold a bird close to my chest without intruding on its space.

> *"Pleasure is the beginning and the end of living happily."*
>
> —Epicurus

130

THINGS TO DO

Trading Pleasure

Start a bulb and seed exchange with friends. When you are doing your harvesting in the fall—dividing bulbs and drying out seeds for next year—try trading with friends for a no-cost way to increase the variety in your garden. We started doing this years ago when we found out the hard way that a packet of zucchini seeds was far too many for two people to plant and eat. We divided them up among our friends around the country and that got the ball rolling.

To send bulbs, place them in a paper bag and then in a box. To collect seeds, shake the flower heads over an empty glass jar. To send seeds, take a small piece of paper and make a little envelope out of it by folding it in half. Take each side and fold in about ½ inch toward middle. Tape those two sides, place the seeds inside the opening at the top and then fold top down and tape again. Write on the outside what is inside and mail in a padded envelope. A sweet surprise for family or friends.

THINGS TO DO

Homemade Herb Vinegars

Before the herbs die back in your garden, why not use them to make homemade vinegars? Packaged in pretty bottles, they make a unique gift. Pick and wash the herbs to be used (sprigs of basil, rosemary, thyme or sage, or a combination all work well). Dry them well on paper towels. Pack the herbs into clean bottles or jars with lids or corks and fill with white wine vinegar. Stand the jars on a sunny windowsill for about two weeks (four weeks if not very sunny). The warmth of the sun will infuse the vinegar with the herbs. Label and decorate the jars with a beautiful ribbon.

131

Garden and the Great Outdoors

Body and Soul

*"I am beginning to learn that it is the sweet, simple things
of life which are the real ones after all."*

—Laura Ingalls Wilder

Small Memories

The grand events on journeys never stay with me—the visit to
the Louvre or the Taj Mahal or Old Faithful. It's the insignificant,
unexpected encounters with people and places that linger in my
memory. A sudden rainbow over a peat bog in the west of Ireland.
The radiant face of a Mayan child giving me directions in Tulum. In
eastern Washington, pausing in evening light to hear the rustle of
ripened heads of wheat, and lifting my gaze to a startling golden
tapestry of wheat rows against a purple haze of mountains. At times
when my life seems difficult, long-forgotten images of delight from
my travels rise unbidden into my consciousness. I never know what's
going to appear next on my memory tapes, and they bring me inde-
scribable pleasure.

"The tragedy of life is not so much what men suffer, but what they miss."

—Thomas Carlyle

Fall Back and Relax

For me, the best day of the year is the last Sunday in October, when we switch from Daylight Savings Time to Standard Time. I deliberately don't set my clock back Saturday night. That way I can bask in the delicious feeling of the extra hour all day Sunday. In the morning I wake up and look at my clock and say to myself, "Oh, no—it's nine o'clock!" But then I remember it's really only eight o'clock and I go back to sleep for an extra hour. All through Sunday I keep thinking it's an hour later than it is. Sometimes I take two or three baths with all this extra time. I finally turn the clock back at bedtime on Sunday night, but only because it wouldn't do to be an hour late for work on Monday.

THINGS TO DO

Get Some Sleep

You can read all the magazine articles you want about stress, anxiety, and exhaustion, but maybe what you need to do is turn out the lights and go to sleep. Experts say we are a sleep-deprived nation and still need between seven and eight hours of sleep a night, no matter how absorbed we are in that new novel or late-night television talk show. Shorten sleeping time, and we lose that most valuable period just before we awaken, when our bodies recharge to deal with stress.

Among the most common advice: Get to bed a half hour earlier than usual and, after a few weeks, add another half hour. Ease toward bedtime with quiet activities such as reading, stretching, meditation. Don't drink caffeine in the evening, or smoke, or drink alcohol before bedtime.

To deal with continual insomnia, one study by a clinical psychologist has come up with dramatically reverse advice: Spend less time in bed to cut down on the frustration of lying awake. Forced to stay awake until, say, one o'clock in the morning, insomniacs drop off to sleep more easily at that time. When they were able to sleep soundly during those limited hours, they gradually extended their time in bed. One more intriguing idea—use the bedroom exclusively for sleep and sex.

135

Body and Soul

$\mathcal{T}$he $\mathcal{D}$rive

When my son was ten, a friend of his died and the ashes were scattered at sea. My son told me he felt sad that there was no place to remember Kevin, and he asked if we could go for a drive around the city waterfront. Several times over the next few weeks, we repeated the memorial drive and used it as a time to think and talk, to cry and remember. Soon this evolved into a comforting ritual of being together that became known as The Drive. Throughout his adolescence, my son often suggested The Drive when we were at loggerheads. On our special route in the protected enclosed space of the car, side by side, it was possible to say things we couldn't have said in another setting, and it helped bring peace between us. When he was older and in despair over breaking up with his girlfriend, we did The Drive again and he used it like a moving therapy session. And now that he's a young adult with his own car, he takes The Drive alone as a way of comforting himself. I think we both know that if there were a personal tragedy of any kind, one of the first things we would do together would be The Drive.

See's Caramel Chocolate with Almonds

It's so big I can just get the whole chocolate in my mouth if I open my jaws wide. I bite down slowly and chew and chew till I'm ready to wash it down with a big mug of Earl Grey tea with cream and really strong honey. I never eat See's with dainty little bites, because taste is only part of the pleasure. There's nothing quite like the sensation of having your teeth sink deeply down through layers of chocolate and caramel and almonds, and you can only get that if you eat the whole thing in one bite. See's are the best, but they're getting hard to find. I drove all the way from Seattle to Vancouver, BC without finding one See's chocolate store, though I went to all the malls where they used to be—it was heartbreaking.

"Eating is heaven."

—Korean proverb

Häagen-Dazs Swiss with Almonds

Sometimes I eat a whole container in one sitting—I think of it as the $4.29 one-serving size. I put the container in my white china jug—the one that came with the tea service I got for my wedding with the red and yellow and blue balloons painted on like an e.e. cummings poem. That way I can eat the ice cream without getting my hands cold and without emptying the container into a bowl. I hold the handle with one hand and a fork with the other. The fork is perfect for digging out the almonds.

Throwing Pots

When I'm throwing pots, they come off the wheel like some-thing alive, with a fine, satiny sheen. Later, when they dry, their luster fades, but for those few special moments they glisten like a lover's skin after making love.

"Beauty is an ecstasy; it is as simple as hunger."

—Somerset Maugham

Saturday Night, Tel Aviv

Once a week in Tel Aviv, the whole city shuts down for twenty-four hours for the observance of Shabbat. No stores, no buses, nothing. And then at sundown Saturday night, there's a sudden explosion into life as everything opens up. Night is coming, but the whole world seems to wake up like Sleeping Beauty, and the city is full of vitality. It's utterly exhilarating. It made me think they should shut things down in cities in North America so that we can experience silence and activity.

THINGS TO DO

A Deep Breath

If you run yourself ragged rushing through the day and seem not to be able to find a time to slow down, take a tip from Vietnamese Buddhist monk Thich Nhat Hahn who recommends that each time the telephone rings, you notice three breaths before you answer. He suggests it as a way to come into an awareness of the present moment, but it is also fabulous for coming back into your body and reducing tension. The more the phone rings, the more relaxed and present you will be!

Orgiastic about Oranges

Body and Soul

One Thanksgiving dinner, my friends and I decided we would each answer the question: "If I were going into the desert and could only take one thing for my comfort, what would it be?" I said my choice would be an orange.

An orange is packed with pleasure in so many different ways. Simply to hold one in your hand is pleasing to the eyes and touch and nose. And when you open it up, you have both thirst-quenching liquid and flavorful food. Everyone has their rituals for peeling an orange. Some people eat the white down beneath the peel, others pick it off. Some bury their face in the flesh and get the juice all over their chin. I prefer the delicate approach, and the mandarin is the best orange for this. First I break it into segments. Then I take an individual segment and bite into the inner part, separating the skin from the flesh. I love the feel of the little moist globules bursting with flavor against my tongue. This is serious pleasure.

*"Black bottom pie is so delicious, so luscious, that I hope
to be propped up on my dying bed and fed a generous
portion. Then I think I should refuse outright to die, for
life would be too good to relinquish."*

—Marjorie Kinnan
Rawlings

140

New School Supplies

Every year when school started, my mom would buy me brand-new school supplies and I'd say to myself, *"This* year I'm not going to screw up. I'm not going to chew my pencils or mess up my exercise books." There was something special about the promise of being able to do it right for once. It was a wonderful feeling that sometimes lasted a week or more. And then one day I'd be on the phone talking about boys and I'd start doodling without even realizing it, or I'd get bored in math class and start sucking my eraser, and my good intentions would be shattered for the rest of the year. I kept making the same resolution right through university, and even though I never kept it past September, I at least had the pleasure of feeling neat and organized a few days each year.

Extolling Espresso

Espresso and reading are complementary pleasures. I look for a place with no music or good music, a place where people stay put for a while and there's not too much commotion. The espresso must be strong and thick so the foam from the coffee sticks to the spoon, and it must be served in small cups. Once I have my coffee in front of me, I take out my book and read extremely slowly, pondering each sentence, perhaps scribbling notes or comments. Poetry or philosophy is best—something that provides pleasure in prose so dense and exquisite that it matches the intensity of the coffee. A single sip of espresso reverberates in my body while the words resonate in my mind with interesting meanings.

141

Body and Soul

> *"A cup of coffee—real coffee—home-brewed, home-ground, homemade, that comes to you dark as a hazel-eye, but changes to a golden bronze as you temper it with cream that never cheated, but was real cream from its birth, thick, tenderly yellow, perfectly sweet, neither lumpy nor frothy on the Java: Such a cup of coffee is a match for twenty blue devils and will exorcise them all."*
>
> —Henry Ward Beecher

Family and Friends

"Have you ever watched children swinging? In order to lift themselves higher . . . they have to dig their toes into the earth."

—Opatoshu

143

Friends and Family

Love of Mincemeat

Twenty-five years ago, when I was in college, I fell in love with a wonderful man and decided to make him a batch of mincemeat cookies on his birthday in November. Now normally I am no baker, and cookies in particular drive me crazy because they take so long—you can't just mix them up and throw them in the oven. Each batch must be carefully watched over to avoid burning and the whole process seems interminable. However, this was love, so I dragged out my mother's recipe, which she made each year around Thanksgiving and gave it the old college try. Well, he loved them—and so did everyone else who tried them.

They became a tradition for me to make at Thanksgiving—one batch for him and one for wherever I was going for Thanksgiving dinner. And, although my love relationship with the man ended a long time ago, we have remained good friends and each year he receives his cookies on November 25, no matter where he is. (Since he's been living on the East Coast and I on the West for the past seven years, they have become the most expensive cookies in the world when Federal Express charges are added in.) In general, I still hate making cookies, but the pleasure I get from pleasing him and the comfort I feel from the continuity of the tradition makes the effort totally worthwhile.

> *"Who has but once dined with friends, has tasted what it*
> *is to be Caesar."*

—Herman Melville

THINGS TO DO

Even if you swear you hate mincemeat, give these a try— they are very tasty and quite unique.

Mincemeat Cookies

1 cup shortening

1½ cups sugar

3 eggs

3 cups unsifted flour

1 teaspoon baking soda

½ teaspoon salt

1½ cups Ready-to-Use Mincemeat (in the jar, not the box; if you buy the boxed kind, follow the recipe on the box because it is drier and proportions are different)

Preheat oven to 375 degrees and grease a baking sheet. In a large bowl, beat shortening and sugar until fluffy. Add the eggs and mix well. Gradually add in the dry ingredients, mixing well after each addition. Stir in mincemeat and combine well. Drop by rounded teaspoonfuls, 2 inches apart, onto baking sheet. Bake 8 to 10 minutes or until lightly browned. For crispy cookies, allow to cool completely before covering; for softer cookies, cover when just slightly cooled. Makes about 6½ dozen.

Friends and Family

The Pleasures of Aging

I gave my sister some money as she had no change, and then I found out I had no money to pay for the parking ticket. A complete stranger came up and said, "How much are you short? I'll come up with it." She called to her husband, "Bert, give her a buck." "You'd do it for somebody else," she whispered to me. If I'd been younger I would have been embarrassed, but I wasn't embarrassed in the least. That's one of the pleasures of old age. I don't get embarrassed and I say whatever I want, no matter how outrageous it sounds, because I just don't care what people think about me. It's not one of the things that really matters in life. I haven't been self-conscious in the least since my mid-seventies.

> *"To be seventy years young is sometimes far more cheerful and hopeful than to be forty years old."*
>
> —Oliver Wendell
> Holmes, Jr.

146

Staying Home from School

Sometimes when I was in grade six or seven and I woke up with a cold or menstrual cramps, I'd tell my mom I was too sick to go to school. She'd make me a soft-boiled egg in a special silver egg-cup. Then came the aspirin and a cozy hot water bottle, and I'd lie back on a comfy pillow with my arm over my eyes. A couple of hours later I'd wake up with the pain gone, and I'd go downstairs and make penuche fudge and get ready for the 1 o'clock movie.

Now came the best part, and that was hearing simultaneously two sounds—the theme song for the 1 o'clock movie and the distant ringing of the school bell six blocks away. We only had one channel, so whatever was on, I'd watch it—if I was lucky it might be a Shirley Temple movie. Because I was sick, I got to eat the fudge right out of the pan, which meant I didn't have to worry about running out. By

around 4 o'clock I'd be all barfy and crampy again, but the pleasure
I'd had made it worthwhile.

Focus on Fudge

Fudge recipes, including those for penuche, abound. The
story goes that fudge is a failed version of some more elegant
confection. Still, it has satisfied generations of youngsters, even
though some cooks find it difficult. Is it too soft to cut into
squares? Too grainy when it's cooled? In this recipe from a
Louisiana kitchen—the pink index card on which it's written
calls it "the best"—a jar of marshmallow cream and a candy
thermometer make the difference. Another recipe calls this
"never-fail fudge." But even a failed fudge is better than no fudge
at all. (This recipe also makes a killer amount, as one of us who
has made it frequently can attest.)

147

*Friends and
Family*

Fabulous Fudge

4½ cups sugar

1 can (14½ ounces) evaporated milk

½ cup (¼ pound) butter

½ teaspoon salt

1 12-ounce Hershey's sweet chocolate bar, chopped

12 ounces semisweet chocolate chips

1 jar (7 ounces) marshmallow cream

1 teaspoon vanilla

2 cups chopped pecans (or walnuts)

In a saucepan over medium heat combine sugar, evaporated milk, butter, and salt. Stirring constantly, bring to a boil and boil 5 more minutes, until a candy thermometer reaches 225 degrees.

Add sweet chocolate, chocolate chips, marshmallow cream, vanilla. Remove from heat and stir until blended and chocolate is melted. Stir in nuts.

Turn into a buttered pan about 10 by 14 by 2 inches. Cool until firm and cut into serving-size pieces. Makes about 4 pounds.

Coming Together

Each year at Thanksgiving, my family and friends do something we call "Appreciations." After we finish eating, we go around the table and say what we value about one another. It's a very simple thing, but it has such a profound effect. In doing it over the years, we've experienced a lot of laughter, many tears of joy, and even some healing of old wounds. It's wonderful to hear what people like about you but a surprising other benefit is seeing what people appreciate in others. Somehow each thing that is said seems to resonate in everyone else, and a lot of "oh yes, I like that, too, but never thought of it"s are registered on the faces around the table.

> *"Do you know that conversation is one of the greatest pleasures in life?"*

> —Somerset Maugham

Ritual of Appreciation

You can do this any time, anywhere. (I've even done it with the fourteen other people in my office, which was an amazing marathon that took three hours!) It's great for bringing people closer together, even those who don't know each other very well (because you can always find something to appreciate about anyone, even if it is the Brussels sprout casserole they contributed to dinner) and really is effective with alienated kids who tend to hear nothing but complaints about them most of the time.

The way Appreciations seems to work best is that one person is chosen first as the focus and then everyone else, as the spirit moves them, speaks about that person. When everyone who wants to has spoken, move on to the next person. There are four rules: remarks must be positive (no sarcasm, backhanded compliments, etc.), no one else may interject anything while someone is speaking, no one has to speak if they don't want to, and the object of the appreciations may not say anything, just take in the praise. It's surprising how difficult the latter is. But you'll get used to it!

A Vote for Cats

I have lived with both cats and dogs, and there are three reasons I take greater pleasure in the company of cats. Cats have no interest in guilt, either for themselves or for their companions. I can feel infuriated with my cat, but I never feel guilty. If I had a dog, it would come up to me and do that thing with its eyebrows that dogs do that means, "You haven't thrown my ball for me. How can you be so insensitive?" A cat would never admit that anything a human does or doesn't do is of any consequence, so there's no cause for guilt at all.

Cats are wonderfully precise, the way they walk around the house or sit with their paws together. This makes the rare moment when they screw up all the more enjoyable, like when Furbl tripped over the phone cord with all four legs and collapsed in a heap and looked at me defensively as if to say, "That wasn't me. That was some other cat."

Cats also can teleport. I first discovered this with Cynthia, whom I'd often find in the living room in the morning, even though I'd locked her in the basement overnight. I found out later that you have to have a tail to do this, because I had a Manx cat who was a total failure at teleporting. Dogs have tails but lack the required concentration.

Guilt-Free Calls

For years, I would never make a long-distance call before eleven at night or after eight in the morning. I was well trained. Then it dawned on me that it was permissible to indulge myself every so often and forget the cheap rates. Now I sometimes make calls in the middle of the day—and I have no qualms about calling back again to mention something I've forgotten. There's nothing nicer than talking to Ingrid in Chicago for an hour and then hanging up and calling her again five minutes later.

> *"It is the friends you can call up at 4 A.M. that matter."*
>
> —Marlene Dietrich

151

Friends and Family

Reading Aloud

Maybe it's because of the storytimes we enjoyed when we were children, but my partner and I have rediscovered how comforting it

is to listen to someone reading aloud. He works at home, and sometimes I feel guilty if I'm just sitting around with a newspaper or magazine. "Read it to me," he says. So I do. I've read bizarre little news
reports and endless magazine articles. We've read to each other: We
finished Gore Vidal's novel, *Burr*, driving between San Francisco and
Los Angeles, alternating behind the wheel. How else are you going
to fill that many miles? And if either one of us is tired of reading, or
tired of listening, we just say so. Out on the patio one afternoon, I
was reading along and discovered he'd fallen sound asleep. I was
reading to the wind. But that's fine—he needed the rest.

> *"The pleasure of all reading is doubled when one lives*
> *with another who shares the same books."*
>
> —Katherine Mansfield

Sensitive New Age Husbands

One of the pleasures of being married twenty years is the way my
husband knows and caters to my smallest pleasures. Like remembering I always take two cubes of ice in my scotch even though he likes
one, and even though it took about 800 times of reminding him.

> *"How simple and frugal a thing is happiness: a glass of*
> *wine, a roast chestnut, a wretched little brazier, the sound*

*of the sea . . . All that is required to feel that here and
now is happiness, is a simple, frugal heart."*

—Nikos Kazantzakis

THINGS TO DO

Say it with Flowers

Instead of a note or letter, consider communicating as the
Victorians did, with flowers. Below is only a small part of the
flower vocabulary:

153

*Friends and
Family*

Chrysanthemum (red)	I love
Clover (white)	Think of me
Daffodil	Regard
Daisy	Innocence
Hibiscus	Delicate beauty
Hollyhock	Ambition
Honeysuckle	Generosity and devotion
Lilac (purple)	First feeling of love
Lilac (white)	Youth, innocence
Magnolia	Love of nature
Mint	Virtue
Pansy	Thinking of you
Parsley	Festivity
Peppermint	Warm feelings

Ranunculus	Charmingly radiant
Rose	Love
Rose (red and white together)	Unity
Rosemary	Remembrance
Sage	Esteem
Sweet basil	Good wishes
Violet	Faithfulness
Zinnia	Thinking of you

154

Nursery Food

I like anything flavorful that I can mush up and eat in small bites. Craig Claiborne calls it "nursery food"—things like porridge and custard that remind people of how they used to eat when they were infants. It's somehow comforting to eat foods in a way that takes you back to your early childhood, when someone was taking loving care of you without asking anything in return. My own favorite nursery food is a scooped-out baked potato covered with melted goat cheese and olive paste and green peas and salad dressing. It gets pretty messy when I start squishing it all over with my fork, but that's the whole point of it. I only do this with people I know well.

THINGS TO DO

A dessert that's best when it looks like a colorful but messy childhood treat is tapioca stirred and folded with almost anything you and your family love to eat. Over the years, family-oriented cookbooks and magazines have suggested dates, bananas, coconut, toasted almonds, berries and—to make it an adult experience—fruit soaked in liqueur. There's even a recipe from the Depression years of the 1930s that calls for grape jelly. And, as a last resort, there's always canned fruit cocktail.

Here's the classic recipe for Minute Tapioca that home economists at Kraft/General Foods revived at a food editor's request. Even the name suggests a mess elevated to celestial status.

Heavenly Hash

1 egg

⅓ cup sugar

2⅓ cups milk

3 tablespoons quick-cooking tapioca

¼ teaspoon salt

1 can (8¼ ounces) crushed pineapple in syrup, drained

8 marshmallows, quartered

1 cup prepared whipped topping, thawed frozen whipped topping, or whipped cream (made from about ½ cup whipping cream)

2 tablespoons chopped maraschino cherries

155

Friends and Family

Beat egg in a large bowl until well blended. Gradually add sugar, beating until thick and lemon colored. Stir in milk, tapioca, and salt. Let stand 5 minutes. Pour into a saucepan.

Cook over medium heat, stirring constantly, 6 to 8 minutes or until mixture comes to a boil. (Pudding thickens as it cools).

Cool 20 minutes. Stir in pineapple and marshmallows. Refrigerate at least 1 hour. Just before serving, stir in whipped cream or topping and cherries. Makes 6 to 7 servings.

156

Breathing Together

One of my greatest pleasures is going to sleep against my lover's back in the spoon position with my arm around him and me breathing in rhythm with him. There's a powerful physiological resonance when I match my breath with his, inhaling at the same time and exhaling just a little longer than he. It's very calming both to him and to me, and it doesn't take many breaths before we fall asleep.

"The flavors are only five in number but their blends are so various that one cannot taste them all."

—Sun-Tzu

THINGS TO DO

There are several good books out about increasing emotional and sexual intimacy through a variety of breathing methods and other simple techniques. Good ones include: *Soulful Sex* by Dr. Victoria Lee, *The Art of Sexual Ecstasy* and *The Art of Sexual Magic* by Margo Anand, and *Sexual Secrets* by Nik Douglas and Penny Slinger.

157

Calming a Child's Fears

Friends and Family

When my daughter was very young, I often had to struggle to find out what was upsetting her. One day, I was walking her to kindergarten and she burst into tears for no apparent reason. It took me a long time to figure out that it was because it was my birthday and she was afraid we'd have a party while she was in school. Another time she got upset when I was teaching her about the solar system. When I talked to her about it, I realized she thought that we were planning to leave Earth and go to another planet. And when we were learning Japanese in preparation for a long stay in Japan, she said to me, "What are we going to speak?" Once I realized that she thought we'd have to stop speaking English altogether, I was able to reassure her.

On occasions like these, I was overwhelmed to feel her fear that was so large that she was afraid to mention what was causing it. Children see the world from a very different place than adults, and problems that seem simple to us are huge to them. It sometimes takes a lot of patience to find out what's bothering them, but it's worth it. The relief that came with putting an end to my daughter's pain was always a source of intense pleasure to me.

"I have reversed the saying of
Troubles are like Babies
the more you nurse them
the bigger They grow
so I have nursed the joys"

—Juanita Harrison

THINGS TO DO

De-stressing Time with Kids

The time you spend with your children may never resemble those cozy, cheerful moments in television commercials for breakfast foods and Christmas toys. And back to school time can be particularly challenging. But there are a few strategies for lowering the stress levels and increasing the pleasure. Focusing on sharing, compromising, and solutions rather than blame may cut back on endless whining and squabbles.

Are mornings a nightmare? Create a half hour in the evening to make lunches, collect books and other items for school, choose clothes for the next day and have them ready. Get kids to bathe or shower.

Is homework a continual struggle? Help your children set up a study area. In the long run, it will pay you to buy them "office" supplies including dictionaries and other reference books. Plan to read, pay bills, answer letters, do your own office "homework" at the same time. Children won't feel that you're enjoying music or television while they're struggling with algebra.

To streamline dinnertime, one woman with teenage children assigned each of them one evening a week to plan the menu and prepare the meal. Whatever the results, at least it spares you from cooking every night. And if it just doesn't work out, there's always breakfast cereal and toast.

Is bedtime an agonizing series of delays? Settle on a time for children to be in bed, then let them read for as long as they like. They may stay awake later than you'd like at first, but at least they're reading, not playing video games. And they should settle into getting the amount of sleep they need.

As always, save "No!" for the really important things. In the long run, your children's clothes and hairstyles won't make much difference. And there's a way to win this argument, eventually: Just take a photograph of them in the styles they insist on wearing and show it to them five years later.

159

Friends and Family

Brief Pleasures

❧

Splitting a hunk of cedar into perfect fragrant strips of kindling on a crisp autumn day and stacking it in neat piles.

A sudden overwhelming awareness of the goodness of another person.

Looking up a word in the dictionary and getting sidetracked by another word. In the 1932 Webster's, in the list of New Words, one finds flivverboob: driver of a flivver.

The sound made by a tennis ball when it smacks the sweet spot.

Making a delicious and nutritious dinner that costs next to nothing.

A cool hand on a fevered brow.

The smell of wood smoke in my hair and clothes after an evening with friends around a beach fire.

The lightness you feel after a long, snowy winter when you get up one morning and you don't have to put on long underwear.

Being asked just the right question by a friend who knows what it is you really want to talk about and opens the way for you.

Fanning out a bridge hand, finding it full of faces and aces, and smiling inside while keeping a straight face.

The momentary ruby flash of a hovering sunlit hummingbird against green trees after a spring rain.

Having the whole family in one bed on a Sunday morning.

Climbing into cold sheets after a hot bath.

The smell of dusty sidewalks after a spring rain, carrying so many exciting aromas I can imagine for a moment what it must be like to have a dog's nose.

The first ride from the airport in a taxi in a strange city halfway round the world late in the evening.

Peeling the wax off a round of cheese.

✂

Winter

China tea, the scent of hyacinths, wood fires and
bowls of violets—that is my mental picture
of an agreeable February afternoon.

—Constance Spry

Home

"Hospitality consists of a little fire, a little food, and an immense quiet."

—Ralph Waldo Emerson

165

Home

That Old Electric-Blanket Feeling

Sometimes on a winter day I get the urge to go for a walk and feel fresh air on my face, but if it's cold and dreary and blowy I often feel like hibernating. That's when I get my electric-blanket feeling. I turn the blanket up high and open the window wide above the head of my bed. When the blanket has warmed up, I climb inside and lie face up so I can feel the wind on my face and smell the salt sea air, while down below I'm warm and snuggly. The contrast is like sweet and sour, or tears and laughter, and it balances my soul. Maybe I'll read a book while the breeze blows across my face. Later I feel like I've gone for a walk but without all the effort. Every time I see an outdoors hot tub my electric-blanket feeling comes, and I remember the pleasure I get from it.

"*The smell of buttered toast simply talked to Toad, and with no uncertain voice, talked of warm kitchens, of breakfasts on bright frosty mornings, of cozy parlor firesides on winter evenings, when one's ramble was over and slippered feet were propped on the fender, of the purring of contented cats, the twitter of sleepy canaries.*"

—Kenneth Grahame,
The Wind in the Willows

166

THINGS TO DO

An easy way to make the house cozy in winter is to use a lot of candles—in the bedroom, living room, dining room, even in the bathroom. They give a nice glow to a dark winter evening and, if scented, also add a soothing fragrance. The nice big pillars can get pretty expensive, but you can cut down on cost and customize your own scent by buying inexpensive, unscented votives, pillars or tea lights at any drugstore, Pier One or Cost Plus. At home, anoint the candle top with a few drops of your favorite essential oil—rose, bayberry, and vanilla are nice—or use a combination that is your unique concoction for a customized and affordable scented candle.

You can also decorate candles with herbs and ribbons. Use large, slow burning candles and attach small sprigs or herbs by using a richly colored ribbon. Be sure to always place candles on fireproof saucers and never leave unattended! And if you want to go even a step further, catalogs like Hearthsong (800-432-6314) even have candle and scent-making kits.

Getting the Most from a Hot Water Bottle

We live in a wood-fired house where not much heat gets to the bedroom. Winter nights, when the woods are dark and silent, it's a pleasure to lie in bed and read. I start preparing about an hour before, by fluffing up the pillows and placing a hot water bottle against the lower pillow, just where my lower back will be when I sit up in bed. Then I lay the old T-shirts that I sleep in over the hot water bottle. When it's time to get into bed, the T-shirt's all warm and so is the pillow against my back. The hot water bottle is now at my feet, all toasty warm, and while I'm reading my back keeps the warmth in the pillow so it's ready to warm up my shoulders when I slide down to go to sleep, enveloped in warmth and coziness.

"I cannot live without books."

—Thomas Jefferson

167

Home

Zap Out Muscle Aches

No hot water bottle or heating pad handy? Try moistening a thick hand towel, or modest-size bath towel, folding it, then heating it in a microwave oven for about 1 minute and 30 seconds. Check to make sure it's not too hot, then press this "moist heat" pad on aching muscles. When it cools down, reheat for about 30 seconds. Use a face towel for smaller aches.

Here's a dry version. Take a clean, heavyweight sock such as a cotton tube sock. Fill halfway with 4-5 cups of raw rice. Tie a knot in the top of the sock or wrap string around it and tie firmly. Warm in the microwave for 30 seconds at a time, until it's the right temperature. It's a heating pad that will fit against sore muscles, especially sore necks. Take care not to get it wet.

A Roaring Fire

We have a great wood-burning stove and most winter days the heat never comes on. There's something elemental about getting wood delivered, stacking it, hauling it in, and building a fire. It takes involvement. Logs have to be added during the evening. Your hands get dirty. It's real. And it's a great way to get the house heated without huge bills.

"Surely everyone is aware of the divine pleasures which attend a wintry fireside: candles at four o'clock, warm hearthrugs, tea, a fair tea-maker, shutters closed, curtains flowing in ample draperies to the floor, whilst the wind and rain are raging audibly without."

—Thomas De Quincey

THINGS TO DO

169

Home

Besides a cheery fire, what is more welcoming on a cold evening than the smell of mulled wine or cider as you come in the door? It is so pleasurable that companies are now selling undrinkable "brews" that you simmer on your stove just for the aroma. Drinkable ones are de rigueur for holiday parties. Great-tasting recipes abound; here are two of our favorites.

Tree-Trimming Cider

16 whole cloves

2 large apples, peeled but left whole

1 gallon apple cider

3 cinnamon sticks

ground nutmeg

Insert 8 cloves into each apple. Pour the cider into a large pot and add the apples and cinnamon sticks. Bring to a boil; then cover and reduce heat to low. Simmer for 1 hour to allow flavors to blend. Discard apples and cinnamon and ladle hot punch into mugs. Sprinkle with nutmeg and serve. Makes 16 servings.

Mulled Wine

2 ¾-liter bottles dry red wine

6 tablespoons sugar

8 whole cloves

4 cinnamon sticks

1 orange, sliced into rounds with peel left on

1 lemon, sliced into rounds with peel left on

1 whole nutmeg, crushed

4 tablespoons rum or cognac, optional

In a large pot over medium high heat, combine all the ingredients except rum or cognac, stirring until sugar is dissolved and the wine is hot but not boiling. Remove from heat and add the rum or cognac, if desired. Let sit for 10 minutes, then remove solids and serve. Makes 8 servings.

A Nest for Sorrow

After my husband died, each significant anniversary—the date of his death, the date of his birth, the date of our wedding anniversary—hit me like a bombshell. I felt like I had to honor the day.

On the first anniversary of his birthday, I got out the feather quilt we got when we were married. It was old and worn, and I took it to a repair shop to have it made smaller for a single bed. The shop was run by an old German woman, rotund, silver-haired, and severe, like a character from a Grimm's fairy tale. She had never said anything personal to me the other times I had been in her store. This time was different. "I know your name," she said, "I know what happened. You must take care of yourself. I'll rebind your feather quilt and you must build yourself a nest. You need a wool mattress pad. You need feather pillows. Build your nest and stay there as long as you need to and as often as you need to." The reason she was so firm with me became apparent as we talked—she explained that she, too, had had a husband who had died, and she had never had time to grieve.

She told me the nest was for sorrow and pain, to comfort the body when the spirit was broken by death. I bought a mattress pad and feather pillows the same day. Every time I went to that store afterwards, the woman was just as she had used to be—professional and businesslike. But the gift she gave me changed my life. I built my nest, just as she suggested, and it helped to heal me.

> *"Love from one being to another can only be that two solitudes come nearer, recognize and protect and comfort one another."*

—Elizabeth Comber

171

Home

Fountain Pens

After years of ballpoints and felt pens, I indulged myself last year by buying a gold-nibbed fountain pen. When I'm getting ready to write a letter, I fill up the pen with royal blue ink that smells exotic and intoxicating. The fat-lacquered middle feels silky smooth against my fingers, and the nib glides across the paper as smooth as butter. The pen is a reminder of some past era of rolltop desks and leather chairs and grandfather clocks, when life was slower and less cluttered, and people took time for reflection when they wrote to a friend.

Letters I write with my fountain pen feel more poetical, more coherent, more intimate. I take time to think about what I'm saying. And when I'm finished, I take pleasure in selecting a stamp that I think the person to whom I'm writing might enjoy. The fact that it takes three or four days to reach her gives me more time to antici- pate the pleasure I hope she'll find in reading my letter. Every time I get another bunch of rushed and disjointed e-mail messages, it strengthens my attachment to leisurely writing and old-fashioned penmanship.

172

> *"The least of things with a meaning is worth more in life than the greatest of things without it."*
>
> —Carl Jung

THINGS TO DO

With most home computers, you can now create your own custom stationery. Try typesetting your name and address in different fonts to discover the right image for you. You can also supply your own artwork—a simple line drawing that you do yourself or find an image in your computer's image file. Then go to your local quick print shop or copy shop, select the right paper and envelopes, and ask their help in reproduction. Voilà! Unique stationery at a fraction of the cost!

173

Home

Sorting Fabric

When I'm feeling fragmented and out of sorts, I go to the room where I keep the bits and pieces of fabric that I'll use some day—all sizes and shapes and colors. I look at each piece, run my hands over the cloth, feel the texture and imagine what I'll do with it; then I sort the pieces. I always feel much more balanced afterwards.

> *"Beauty of style and harmony and grace and good rhythm depend on simplicity."*
>
> —Plato

Other Handiwork

For an elegant gift, try making bookmarks out of ribbons and beads. Choose a pretty ribbon that's at least an inch wide, velvet and tapestry styles are nice. Trim the top with pinking shears to keep it from raveling. Fold up the end of the ribbon to make a point. Tack the ends together with a couple of secure stitches in a matching thread. Sew a bead or charm onto the end of the point to weight the bookmark and add a pretty accent.

A New Mattress

I've got a brand new mattress, the first new one I've ever had. All my life I've slept on futons and foamies and dreamed of the pleasure of a real mattress, and now I've got one, and a new down duvet I can pull over my head and know I'm going to be warm at night. What a relief! Now I wonder why I slept so long on futons and foamies. It's like hitting your head on a wall over and over again because you know it'll feel so good when you stop.

> *"Your body is the ground metaphor of your life, the expression of your existence. It is your Bible, your encyclopedia, your life story. Everything that happens to you*

is stored and reflected in your body. Your body knows;
your body tells. The relationship of your self to your
body is indivisible, inescapable, unavoidable. In the
marriage of flesh and spirit, divorce is impossible . . ."

—Gabrielle Roth

Flannel Sheets

175

Home

The best thing about long prairie winters is coming in from working on the farm on a bitter blowy day and jumping into bed and being enveloped by fuzzy flannelette sheets. It doesn't matter how cold it is in the house, the minute I hit those sheets I'm warm.

My wife believes in the prophetic power of ritual. Every year on April 1, she changes the bed and puts on cotton summer sheets. This is her way of welcoming summer back. The only problem is that summer isn't there to be welcomed in April. It's still halfway winter, and the cotton gives me goosebumps. Finally summer comes, and it gets hot for a few weeks, and then there's the harvest moon and the first frost. To my mind, this is the logical time to get the flannel sheets back on quick, so we can get ready for the first blizzard. No such luck. My wife maintains that Thanksgiving is the real end of summer and the beginning of flannel sheets.

On just about everything else we see eye to eye, but on this issue we're stuck. I've read those books on how men and women can communicate better, but none of them mentions that women are more hot-blooded and can't understand why flannel sheets are so important to men.

> *"Year by year the complexities of this spinning world*
> *grow more bewildering and so each year we need all the*
> *more to seek peace and comfort in the joyful simplicities."*

—Women's Home
Companion,
December 1935

176

THINGS TO DO

Catalog Shopping

Before electronic gadgets and polyester clothing, mail-order catalogs offered sensible, basic goods to improve quality of life. Some of them still do:

The Vermont Country Store in Weston concentrates on items that are no longer available but were once popular and useful. This kind of merchandise fills a need, not because it's nostalgic, but because it worked and kept on working. In its catalog you'll find nightshirts; all-cotton sheets; chenille bedspreads; badger shaving brushes; thick, hotel-quality bath towels; garden weeding tools, and a variety of old-fashioned soaps and health remedies. For a catalog, call (802-362-2400).

The Cumberland General Store in Crossville, Tennessee seems like a time machine. Its catalog includes old-style kitchenware, such as soapstone griddles and coffee percolators, a handmade Amish rocking chair, hard-to-find cakes of Bon Ami cleanser, toy wooden tops and wire puzzles, kits for re-caning chairs, dulcimers—and even a ready-to-assemble windmill. Call (800-334-4640). And L.L. Bean of Freeport, Maine, may have edged into the mainstream, but the catalog is still a good place to shop for handsewn moccasins, warm flannel sheets, and Adirondack chairs. Call (800-221-4221).

177

Home

Oat Bran Cereal

To fully savor oat bran cereal, it's important to start with a bowl with a pretty pattern. Mine has painted cranberries. In it I put three separate piles: hot oat bran cereal, cold yogurt, and apple sauce. I'm very careful not to mush them up. That makes it possible to get a little bit of each in my spoon and keep them separate. That way I can taste the hot, the sour, and the sweet together—three flavors, three temperatures, three textures. The contrast inside my mouth is wonderful. And to add to the pleasure, I have the delight of gradually revealing the pattern of painted cranberries as I make my way through the cereal.

"The full use of taste is an act of genius."

—John La Farge

THINGS TO DO

This is a nineteenth century confection that, when placed in a dainty box lined with tissue paper, makes a great housewarming or holiday gift.

Homemade Orange or Lemon Peel

2 quarts plus 1 cup bottled water (cannot use tap water)

2 tablespoons kosher salt

rind from 10 navel oranges or 15 lemons, cut into halves or quarters

4 cups granulated sugar

superfine sugar

Combine 1 quart of water with the salt in a medium saucepan and bring to a boil. Boil for 5 minutes and set aside. When cool, pour into a large jar, add the rinds, cover and store in refrigerator for 6 days.

Pour the brine into a kettle and bring to a boil. Reduce heat, add rinds and poach for 10 minutes. Drain rinds thoroughly in a strainer and discard liquid.

Combine 1 quart of water and 2 cups sugar. Bring to a boil, add rinds and boil for 30 minutes or until peel starts to look clear around the edges. Drain rinds in colander.

Cut rinds into strips. Combine remaining 1 cup water and 2 cups sugar. Bring to a boil and add rinds. Boil gently until syrup candies on the strips. Remove the strips with a slotted spoon and spread them to dry on racks. Drying time will vary depending on weather, but usually takes a day. When strips are dry, dust lightly with superfine sugar and store in airtight containers. Makes 1 pound.

179

THINGS TO DO

Dried Flower Decorations

Home

Anyone who has ever had a Christmas tree has probably made paper, popcorn, or cranberry chains and perhaps even more elaborate handmade ornaments. One simple and elegant way to decorate a Christmas tree is with small bunches of dried flowers. They are very easy to make and, if stored carefully— don't crush—will last year after year. You can use almost any dried flowers, but try a combination of lavender, fresh rosemary, baby's breath, roses, and statice. First cut each flower into small sprigs and place in separate piles. Lay two or three sprigs of rosemary on the table. Add a sprig of baby's breath, then a few roses and statice. Tie the stems together with florists' wire (leaving a length of wire long enough to attach the spray to the tree), so that the stems are tight and the flowers fan out at the top. If you want a scent, sprinkle a few drops of an essential oil.

These can also be used to decorate mirrors, picture frames, or place settings.

Natural Nuances

Give a special touch to your table with unique, and easy placecards. For inspiration look to the great outdoors! Collect small pinecones, berry clusters, crab apples, pretty leaves, or other natural ornaments. Create a card for each guest, and use a pretty ribbon or piece of raffia to attach the cards to your natural treasures. Place one at each setting.

It is the simple things of life that make living worthwhile, the sweet fundamental things such as love and duty, work and rest, and living close to nature.

—Laura Ingalls Wilder

Garden and the Great Outdoors

"He that plants a tree loves others besides himself."

—English proverb

181

Garden and the
Great Outdoors

The Ultimate Mud Pie

The first week of January, when the rain is pouring down in buckets, I set aside a day to get out in the garden in my rubber boots and my most disreputable clothes. This is the time of year when the compost box looks its worst—a bulging mix of leaves, twigs, weeds, flower stalks, and kitchen waste, all soggy and far too cold to decay. I take the biggest fork I can lay my hands on and take the slats off the box and fork the whole mess onto the ground. Then I make separate piles of other ingredients: a dozen garbage bags of horse manure, ripe, pungent, and full of promise; a heap of sea lettuce, dragged up from the beach after the November storms; a pile of ordinary dirt. Then comes the best part: piling it all together in layers like a really gooey Black Forest cake, except with manure instead of cherries.

By now, I'm covered in dirt and rain and bits of seaweed, and I'm sliding around in the muck and having the time of my life, though anybody else might think I was doing an unpleasant chore. Finally I cover the new compost heap up in black plastic and head indoors for the hottest bath I can stand.

And then comes the moment of greatest pleasure: the sunny day in February when I peel back the plastic and smell the rich odor of decay and see the warm steam rising. A fork plunged into the pile reveals my greatest hope come true: a mass of seething worms, working their little hearts out to turn my compost pile into rich black soil. There's no magic like it.

182

> *"A house with daffodils in it is a house lit up, whether or no the sun be shining outside. Daffodils in a green bowl—and let it snow if it will."*
>
> —A.A. Milne

THINGS TO DO

Coaxing Spring

When you've got the winter blahs, say around February or March, one of the easiest cures is to anticipate spring by forcing branches to bring a bit of color indoors. Any of a wide variety of bushes, shrubs, and trees will do, including forsythia, crab apple, pussy willows, quince, cherry, plum, pear, dogwood, privet, red maple, gooseberry, weeping willow, and witch hazel. Simply cut the edges of the branches on a slant with sharp scissors and plunge immediately into a vase of warm water. As the days pass, make sure there is plenty of clean tepid water in the vase and the warmth of the house will do the rest of the work. Voila, instant spring!

The Delights of Fantasy

Winter can be hard on gardening fanatics, forced indoors to attend only to the houseplants. So I always cheer myself up by collecting all the bulb and seed catalogs that come throughout the year and saving them for a dreary January weekend. I sit down at the kitchen table with them all spread out in front of me. First I pore over the beautiful color pictures and the accompanying descriptions, fantasizing about the incredible garden I could have if money, time, and weather conditions were no object: Shirley tulips "ivory white with purply pictee edge," a one-of-a-kind Batik Iris that has "dramatic white spatters and streaks against a royal purple ground," Alboplenum, "doubly rare for being both multi-petaled and white."

After I have completely satisfied my eyes, I get real. I make a map of my vegetable and flower gardens, check out what seeds I have left from last year and plot out what I want to plant. Then I go

183

Garden and the
Great Outdoors

back over the catalogs again with a more selective eye and choose what I really need. Often this process goes over many days and both parts give me great pleasure: the indulging of my wildest gardening fantasies and the anticipation of color, beauty, and form in my actual garden.

"If I had but two loaves of bread, I would sell one and buy hyacinths, for they would feed my soul."

—The Koran

184

THINGS TO DO

Great gardening catalogs abound. Good general ones include: Park Seed (800-845-3369), The Seed Catalog (800-274-7333), and The Cook's Garden (802-824-3400). More specialized ones include: Tomato Growers Supply Company (813-768-1119), Native Seed/SEARCH (602-327-9123), and our personal favorite, Shepherd's Garden Seeds (in the East, 860-482-3638; in the West, 408-335-6910), which has a wide selection of unusual, easy to grow, disease-resistant vegetables, and lots of old-fashioned flower strains.

Snow Bunny

I love winter. For me, there is nothing like the day after a big blizzard when the sun comes out. I bundle up and head outside. The sun on the sparkling snow, the deep quiet that only snow creates, the cold air on my cheeks—absolutely nothing else makes me feel so alive. I walk and walk, happy simply to be alive.

185

THINGS TO DO

Tractor Tracks

After the first big blizzard of winter ends and the snow is clean and white, go out and make tractor tracks. Walk with your feet pointing out at a 45-degree angle. First you put your left foot down, and then you put your right foot down so your heel's against the middle of your left foot, and then it's left, right, left till it looks just like a John Deere's been passing through on the way to the barn. Don't forget to do both wheels, if you really want to impress your mom. To impress your kids, you may need to add a snow angel between the tracks. Just lie on your back and wave your arms back and forth in the snow. Get up carefully without stepping on your imprint. Admire your handi-work.

Garden and the Great Outdoors

THINGS TO DO

This is a great nineteenth century treat that you can replicate if you live in snowy climes.

Snow Ice Cream
1 cup heavy cream
¼ cup superfine sugar
2 teaspoons lemon extract or two tablespoons rosewater
8 to 10 cups fresh, clean snow

Mix the cream, sugar, and lemon extract or rosewater. Add the snow, beating with a whisk, using only enough snow to make a stiff ice cream. Serve immediately. Makes 8 servings.

Indoor Greenery

When it's gray and dreary outside, I like to plant an indoor "kitchen garden" in the sunny window of my apartment. One of my favorites is a lemon herb garden because it lends such a tart fragrance to the room. That lemony smell keeps me going all winter.

"Green fingers are the extensions of a verdant heart."

—Russell Page

THINGS TO DO

Making an indoor herb garden is easy. You can either put plants in one long container or use a variety of small pots. Choose from lemon basil, lemon verbena, lemon thyme, lemon balm, lemon geranium, and lemongrass to fill the air with the delicious, tangy scent of citrus. Treat these plants to plenty of sun and well-drained soil. Be sure to pick the blooms off of lemon verbena and lemon basil. The more you pick and use these herbs, the more prolific the plants will be. Consider mixing in a yellow flowering plant to visually highlight the lemon fragrance.

What to do with all this lemon flavor? Try making lemon honey: Coarsely chop ½ cup lemon balm or lemon verbena and place in a saucepan with 1 cup honey. Over low heat, cook for 20 minutes, then strain out herbs and store honey in a container with a tight lid. Or make lemon butter: Soften ½ cup butter and mix in 2 tablespoons of finely chopped lemon basil or lemon thyme. Great for seafood and pasta.

187

Garden and the Great Outdoors

Body and Soul

"Whenever you are sincerely pleased you are nourished."

—Ralph Waldo Emerson

189

Body and Soul

A Good Cry

Sometimes there is just nothing like a good cry. In my day-to-day existence, I've found that it is so easy to let life encrust me until I wake up one day and notice that there is a calcified shell over my heart, "protection" against the slights of friends, the grind of commuting, the sight of a filthy homeless woman picking through garbage on the corner. Somehow even though I know that the shell is keeping me away from my own truest self, away from my deepest capacity to love, there is nothing I seem to be able to do about cracking it open, breaking it apart. Then, miraculously, some small thing makes its way through the shell—a particularly sad movie, the suffering of a loved one, a fight with my husband—and the floodgates of tears open.

Crying itself is no picnic—the red eyes, the heaving sobs—but the feeling afterwards! It's the sensation of having been completely emptied out, cleansed of all the detritus accumulated by living in the modern world, reconnected to a heart that is willing, once again, to feel. Over and over I relearn the same lesson: it is through pain I am brought again to joy and only through emptiness can I experience fullness.

> *"In the beginning nothing comes.*
> *In the middle nothing stays.*
> *In the end nothing goes."*
>
> —Milarepa

190

In a Lather

I don't know how my father's shaving brush found its way to my medicine cabinet. I don't even remember him ever using it—when I watched him shaving, he had switched to the "modern" aerosol shaving foams that fizzed out of the cans. But here it is—a brush with a sculpted base that looks like an early plastic version of ivory, rigid bristles ("pure bristles—sterilized—made in England") the label explains. There's another tiny label with the maker's shield and a pair of prancing griffins, those ancient symbols of protection. In the morning, my face needs all the protection it can get.

When I dared to use the shaving brush myself—it seemed almost too personal—I was amazed at how comforting it made this morning ritual. Giving it a blast of hot water, then swirling it around a cake of shaving soap, I discovered that the brush did all the work. A catalog from Caswell-Massey, which proclaims itself America's oldest chemists and perfumers, explained the theory and practice. "We cannot imagine," these chemists said, "why anyone would consider it progress to abandon a brush for shaving." They went on to explain that the brush lifts and separates each hair of the beard, coats it with lather, and softens the skin. Who could imagine those pungent-smelling shaving gels, like so much lime marmalade, doing all that?

The shaving soaps are another pleasure, with evocative names and agreeable fragrances like sandalwood, almond, and verbena. I discovered that shaving with a brush feels cool in the summer—you don't have to drench your face with hot water—and warm and comforting in the winter. And at any time of the year, it's a pleasure to leave the house in the morning with one satisfying accomplishment behind you.

> *"Everything should be made as simple as possible, but not simpler."*
>
> —Albert Einstein

191

Body and Soul

THINGS TO DO

A great source of shaving brushs, soaps and lotions is Escential Lotions and oils. (800-750-6457). They have wonderful gift baskets too.

Old-fashioned Bathtubs

We have an old clawfoot bathtub that's designed for the human body—deep and rounded, with a sloping back. Something has gone amiss with the design of modern bathtubs. They're short and shallow and designed to put a crick in your back if you relax. Bathtub designers are under the mistaken impression that bathtubs are for cleaning the body. They're not. If I want to get clean, I'll stand in the shower, where I can do it right.

Bathtubs are for pleasure. They're for lying back and getting books wet while you read. They're for lighting a candle and contemplating the flame while you ruminate on pleasant memories and improbable fantasies. They're for entertaining cats, for whom watching naked bodies in water is the next best thing to wet food. They're for submersing your whole body so your knees don't stick out in the cold air while you hum "Some Enchanted Evening" with your head underwater. And on special occasions they're for making love and slopping water all over the floor. That's what bathtubs are for.

*"There must be quite a few things a hot bath won't cure,
but I don't know any of them."*

—Sylvia Plath

Taking the Waters

For a relaxing bath, add lavender or chamomile oil to running water. Start with ¼ teaspoon for a whole tub of water. For scents to inspire your sensuality, try ¼ teaspoon of sandalwood, ylang ylang, or cinnamon essential oils.

For an invigorating bath, try clipping a few pieces of fresh rosemary from your garden (or buy them at the grocery store). Take a piece of cheesecloth, tulle, or fine netting, and tie the rosemary up in it with a piece of twine or thread. Pound it with a mallet to release the oils. Hold the "sachet" under warm running water, then let it float in the bath.

193

Body and Soul

A Free Vacation

When my husband is away, I sometimes spend the night in the guest bedroom in the old-fashioned double bed I used before I was married. It has a fluffy comforter, ruffled pillow shams, and pretty sheets. If I adjust the miniblinds just right, I get a lovely view of the treetops and city lights, instead of the tar-and-gravel rooftops and power lines I see during the day. And because there is only one outlet in the room, just enough for a lamp and a clock, I read in bed rather than watch TV. Spending the night in the guest room makes me feel as though I'm staying at a bed and breakfast inn.

> *"Ah! There is nothing like staying at home for real comfort."*
>
> —Jane Austen

194

THINGS TO DO

Bath Salts

You can feel great by making bath salts for yourself or for gifts. In a large bowl, place 3 cups Epsom salts. In a measuring cup, combine 1 tablespoon glycerin, a couple drops of food coloring, and a spray of your favorite perfume. Mix well and then slowly add the liquid mixture to the Epsom salts, stirring well. Pour into decorative glass jars and tie on a ribbon bow.

Imagined Photographs

I like to imagine ordinary, everyday scenes as photographs. Any scene will do: the view from the Walterdale Bridge on an ice-fogged day when all you can see is the dark movement of the unfrozen thread of water through the mist; the desolate stretch of strip mall and lube shops as you travel a suburban artery; a herd of ugly lamps dangling clearance tags in a department store. I take a great deal of pleasure imagining these things contained in a photographic frame, rendered iconographic through the loss of a dimension.

> *"There is no pleasure in having nothing to do; the fun is in having lots to do and not doing it."*
>
> —Mary Wilson Little

195

Body and Soul

THINGS TO DO

A Tiny Perfect Picture Frame

You're eight years old and you have the perfect present for your grandpa—a picture of you. The only problem is, the frame needs to be small because you're not very big in the photo and you want to cut out the head of your sister standing next to you.

Worry no more. The solution is as close as the hardware store or your local craft store. Get one wooden curtain ring that's just the size you need, some string that you just know is your grandpa's favorite color, and some clear glue. Glue one end of the string to the curtain ring and wind the string tightly all the way around the ring till you get to the place you started from. Cut the string there and glue the loose end to the ring. Then glue on a little loop of string to hang the frame on a wall or a fridge, cut a circle out of the photo the exact same size as the ring, and glue it to the back.

Now you have the perfect present. Remind your grandpa repeatedly that you made it all by yourself, and help him pick a place to display it so he can see your face every day.

The Blizzard Bath

When it's dark and stormy outside in the early morning on workdays, I get out of my warm bed and start running my bath and go downstairs in my nightie. I put on my old boots with the fuzzy insides (which I never wear for anything else) and an old coat so I still have all my bed-warmth with me, and I go out into the blizzard in my bed-warmth and start my car. I get colder and colder in my car while the bed-warmth fades away, but I'm imagining my bath getting warmer and warmer. Sometimes after I get out of my car I sweep the snow off the sidewalk so I can get a little bit colder still and know I deserve my bath because I've done a chore. I love the feel of the wind whipping around my bare legs and the strange looks people give my mussed-up bed-hair. Then I run upstairs and throw off my clothes and slide my cold body into the deliciously hot bath.

"Nothing can cure the soul but the senses, just as nothing can cure the senses but the soul."

—Oscar Wilde

THINGS TO DO

Herbal baths

Many stores and catalogs offer wonderful "tub teas," collections of herbs packed in oversize teabags to drop in the bathtub while it fills, and if you are feeling ambitious, you can even make your own. Simply tie together a few bags of an herbal tea you like to the tap. Or fill a tea infusion ball with herbs, or tie up herbs in a double thickness of cheesecloth. You can even use the foot of a clean nylon stocking. Afterward, you can let the bag dry (be careful where it drips) and use it for a few more baths. Alternatively, pour a pint of boiling water over dried or fresh herbs, steep for 10 minutes, then strain into the tub.

A variety of herbs is available at stores specializing in natural foods and remedies. Here are some traditional combinations. For a relaxing bath: chamomile, jasmine, hops. For a stimulating bath: marigold, lavender, bay, mint, rosemary, thyme. Healing bath: calendula, comfrey, spearmint.

197

Body and Soul

Warm Towels

Before I get into the shower, I put a big, fluffy bath towel in the dryer. When I get out of the shower, while I dry myself with another towel, my wife gets the hot towel out of the dryer and wraps it around my shoulders. It's a wonderful feeling, being completely enclosed in dry, soft warmth after being wet all over. I've heard of people who sprinkle a little water on a towel and heat it in the microwave, but my towel's too big for that. It has to be huge for maximum comfort.

THINGS TO DO

Refresh your Bathroom

If you use a room deodorizer, you don't need to throw it away as the scent begins to wane. Simply put a few drops of your favorite perfume on top of it and it will continue to scent the air.

Recipe for a Relaxed Evening

At the end of a long day at work cutting people's hair, I've got sensory overload and need to clear my mind and body. When I get home I want to be with people but not have to make contact. First I get my body comfy. I put on my holster pants and my fuzzy-on-the-inside, stylish-on-the-outside sweatshirt. Then I mix a hot buttered rum (if it's winter) and make up a plate of crackers and smoked salmon, just for me, nobody else. Then I move to the living room and watch *Wheel of Fortune*. The mindlessness of it mellows me out for the evening, and the crackers and salmon take the edge off my hunger. It's like going to the gas station for a fill-up and putting in a little high-grade oil. Then I'm ready to be with people again. This is my after-work ritual, and if anything interrupts it, the evening just isn't right. If someone calls late in the afternoon for a 5:30 appointment, I just think of 7 o'clock and *Wheel of Fortune* and calm right down.

199

Body and Soul

"*Taking joy in life is a woman's best cosmetic.*"

—Rosalind Russell

THINGS TO DO

There are many ways to pamper yourself when you get home from work. One very simple one is to change out of work clothes and anoint yourself with an essential oil. One of our favorites is a combination we call Vamber. Pour equal parts of amber and vanilla essential oils into a vial. Shake well. The result is a uniquely rich and sensual combination that is both comforting and sexy—perfect for the evening.

Stolen Moments

When you are a busy parent of young children, there is nothing more wonderful than a few stolen moments of peace and quiet. I have a friend with six kids whose true pleasure in life is locking herself in the bathroom for five minutes of (hopefully) uninterrupted private time. For me, a voracious reader, one of the hardest things about being a mother was not having any time to read before the kids were asleep. By the time I got them to bed, I was so exhausted I fell asleep with my book in hand.

I remember vividly the day that my now eighteen-year-old daughter learned to tell time. She was the kind of kid who needed constant interaction and immediately pounced on me whenever she saw me settle on the bed or couch with a book in my hand. But the day I knew she could tell time, I said, "Mummy needs to lie here and read a book for thirty minutes so you need to go play by yourself. When the big hand gets on the six, you may come back and I will stop reading." She did it and that thirty minutes were heaven. And while I must have used the trick many other times, I can only recall the deep-down cellular happiness from that first time—reading in daylight, what a delicious treat.

"Only one hour in the normal day is more pleasurable than the hour spent in bed with a book before going to sleep, and that is the hour spent in bed with a book after being called in the morning."

—Rose Macaulay

The Healing Poncho

When I was sick with chronic fatigue syndrome, my body's thermostat went on the fritz. I was often very cold, but I hated to have the heat high and make other people in the house too hot. Then a friend gave me a thickly woven, long, reversible poncho— purple and cobalt on one side and just purple on the other. When I felt cold, I put it on and used it like a healing blanket. Not only did it make me warm, but whenever I wore it, I felt positively queenlike, swathed in purple and blue, even though there was only a little sick body in a nightgown underneath. When I was wearing the poncho it entirely changed my image of myself, and helped me feel stronger and healthier.

201

Body and Soul

Silk Scarves

A colleague once asked me why I always wear scarves. I explained that my neck often gets cold and uncomfortable, and that

I simply like the feel of silk. "That's amazing," she said. "I only wear a scarf if it goes with my outfit." I said I'd rather pick a comfortable and beautiful scarf and not worry about the outfit. This made her stop and think. She told me she often has a cold neck but had thought she had to put up with discomfort if it meant having an acceptable look.

The beauty of silk scarves is that they not only have a wonderful texture and warmth, but their rich colors can make me feel better even if I never see myself in the mirror. Wearing them adds to the quality of my life and helps me do my job better. Some things I can put up with, but a cold neck isn't one of them.

"Only the heart knows how to find what is precious."

—Dostoevsky

Paris Crepes

My fondest memory of Paris is of cold, miserable, rainy days when I'd treat myself to a *beurre sucré* from a sidewalk vendor. This was a delicate sugared crepe, rolled up and wrapped in wax paper to keep it warm. I'd walk along watching the street life and nibbling the crepe while the warm, sugary butter ran down my arm, mingling with the raindrops. The bitterness of the day somehow intensified the pleasure of the taste of the crepe, and the warmth and sweetness were a comfort against the weather. The crepes tasted best when shared with a lover, though they also compensated excellently for his absence if there was no lover in my life that day.

Revival of the Martini

203

Body and Soul

If, as Clifton Fadiman wrote, cheese is milk's leap toward immortality, then the martini is gin's reaching respectability. In Hollywood's *Thin Man* movies of the 1930s, William Powell and Myrna Loy gave the martini wit and sophistication. In the James Bond movies, Sean Connery and a parade of other actors gave it character and masculinity. Old stories of "gin mills" and "bathtub gin" recede into distant memory. Maybe it's the glass that does it: If it's tall, elegant and slim—why, we must be, too!

The martini is truly a simple pleasure—nothing more than gin and vermouth, maybe an olive or a twist of lemon peel. But those few ingredients have generated uncounted arguments, cartoons, double-takes in Broadway comedies, and silly jokes printed on cocktail napkins. For years, the drink went out of favor, but happily, it has recently enjoyed a comeback, with everyone and his brother offering their own slight variation.

The dark ages of the martini were literally that: It was a sweet drink made with gin and sweet, dark Italian vermouth.

Dry vermouth eventually replaced it, and martinis have been getting drier ever since.

Just to see what progress we've made, try making a traditional martini with 3 parts gin and 1 part dry vermouth. A dry martini is 4 to 7 parts gin, 1 part vermouth. An extra dry martini, gin in any proportion and a dash—or a mere hint—of vermouth. Pour it over cracked ice, stir until it's chilled, strain into martini glasses.

Green olives, plain or stuffed, garnish basic martinis and dry martinis. (Trader Vic Bergeron, who made his martinis with rum instead of gin, insisted on rinsing the olives to remove the salty brine.) The extra-dry martini takes a strip of lemon peel (twisted over the glass but not dropped into it.)

> *"I must get out of these wet clothes and into a dry martini."*
>
> —Alexander Woolcott

Friends and Family

"To see a World in a Grain of Sand
And Heaven in a Wild Flower,
Hold Infinity in the palm of your hand
And Eternity in an hour."

—William Blake

205

The Stuffed Animal Support Group

My stuffed animals are a pleasure to me just by being who they are and by always being there, stalwart and faithful, when I need them. They each have special tasks to bring me comfort where and when I most need it.

I'm of an age now that when I lie on my side, there's a soft beach-ball where my flat tummy used to be, and Saul the polar bear acts as a supplementary pillow to hold up the fort there and protect my lower back. He's just a soft white teddy, but that's his job and that's what he does best.

Sebastian is a brown bear, and he doubles as an extra under the head pillow, and Abigail the bunny uses her floppy ears to soothe my eyes and keep out the light.

Last but not least is Thomas Fitzroy the River Bear. He's just a little hand-sized bear with a wee fisherman's sweater, but he's the bravest of all. When I went rafting on the Colorado River, I held him on my stomach in my sleeping bag, and over my heart when I was scared in the rapids. He also assisted others on the trip, including some sophisticated big-city women who didn't know about teddy bears in terms of comfort.

I think of teddies as angels with fur—always good-natured and supportive purveyors of comfort and safety.

"Simplicity is the whole secret of well-being."

—Peter Matthiessen

THINGS TO DO

Foolproof Cake

Maybe you're a good cook, but you still tell yourself you're not a good baker. The cookies and brownies turn out all right, but the lopsided birthday cake was a joke and you're still telling the story of the angel food cake you balanced upside down on the wine bottle to cool, and . . .

But anyone can make a pineapple upside-down cake, and nobody can turn down a serving. It's always comforting food that recalls the childhood surprise of a plain cast iron skillet revealing a steaming cake topped with jewel-like pineapple slices and cherries and nuts. And the intense pleasure of dipping a finger in the caramelized brown sugar when it was still too hot to touch.

Note: a packaged mix, the size for a single-layer or loaf cake, may be used instead of the homemade batter. The pineapple and brown sugar will get all the attention anyway.

Pineapple Upside-Down Cake

¼ cup (½ stick) butter

¾ cup packed brown sugar

7 canned pineapple rings, drained

7 maraschino cherries

½ cup pecans or walnuts

⅓ cup shortening

⅔ cup granulated sugar

1 teaspoon vanilla

2 eggs

1⅔ cups all-purpose flour

2 teaspoons baking powder

¼ teaspoon salt

⅔ cup milk

Preheat oven to 350 degrees. Melt butter in a 9- or 10-inch cast iron or other ovenproof skillet. Sprinkle in the brown sugar and cook over medium heat, stirring, until melted and bubbling.

207

Friends and Family

Remove from heat. Arrange pineapple slices in the bottom of the pan, with a cherry in the center of each slice. Fit nuts in between.

In a large bowl, cream shortening with granulated sugar. Add vanilla and eggs and beat until fluffy. Stir together flour, baking powder, and salt. Add flour mixture to the creamed mixture alternately with the milk, beating until batter is smooth.

Carefully spoon the batter over the pineapple slices. Bake in oven for 35 to 45 minutes, until a skewer inserted in the center comes out clean. Remove from oven and let stand for 5 minutes. Place a serving plate face down over skillet. Using pot holders or oven mitts to protect hands, turn both upside down and remove the skillet.

A Dog's Best Friend

My sister likes to put her boyfriend's feet on her lap and rub them. She says it calms her. And I calm myself by rubbing my dog, feeling his soft warm body and fur and watching his ecstasy. There's something special about being able to give pleasure in a safe way to another being. With humans it can turn into something else, something more complicated, but dogs have no expectations.

"Our perfect companions never have fewer than four feet."

—Colette

The Pleasure of Giving Pleasure

Many people don't seem to have a clue about how to make themselves comfortable when they're feeling bad. They seem resigned to being in a not-good place. Maybe they feel too busy, or maybe they think they'll look unconventional if they put on a blanket or a scarf to be warm.

I don't accept that. I'd rather look unacceptable than be uncomfortable, and it gives me pleasure to make others comfortable too. If someone comes over for dinner and feels cold or sick, I'll give them a hot water bottle even if they're all dressed up, or I'll throw a blanket over their shoulders or give them a delicious glass of juice with vitamin C in it. I also like to expose people to music that will give them pleasure, and I select it according to their mood. The second movement of Beethoven's Seventh Symphony can pull me from the depths of despair to standing up with my arms in the air and I like to share that experience.

> "That it will never come again is what makes life so sweet."
>
> —Emily Dickinson

209

Friends and Family

Toi and Moi Jamaica Joy Juice Massage Lotion

A good massage is a fabulous pleasure to give someone else and it requires a good lotion. This formula was developed by Andy Bryner, a connoisseur of simple pleasures, over a ten-year period. It was first produced in Vermont, then modified in Florida and Hawaii to suit more tropical climes. Because the oils contain no preservatives, it's best to mix small quantities at a time to prevent spoilage. This recipe is for 1 quart. Good suppliers of oil are Attar Herbs and Spices in New Ipswich, NH (800-541-6900) or Frontier Cooperative Herbs in Norway, Iowa (800-669-3275).

(If you would prefer something that is a bit less ambitious, try putting 1 tablespoon of your favorite essential oil in 6 ounces of unscented store-bought lotion. Citrus, gardenia, raspberry, or a combination of cucumber and ivy are all quite nice.)

Mix together the following in a large bowl then pour into smaller plastic containers:

30 ounces organic peanut, safflower, or olive oil or, for a less greasy feel in tropical climates, 10 ounces of the above oils

plus 20 ounces commercial moisturizing lotion (for example, Marley, Mill Creek, Jasons, Prime), preferably with Apricot scent

4 eyedroppers Oil of Sweet Orange

2 eyedroppers Oil of Bay

2 eyedroppers Oil of Lime

1½ eyedroppers Oil of Lemon

1 eyedropper Oil of Bitter Almond

½ eyedropper Oil of Apricot

secret ingredient

This recipe, he writes, calls for a secret ingredient that you will have to add on your own. Use imagination to find yours; it should symbolize loving, fragrant, delight and joy at being alive in a body.

211

A Heart-Felt Valentine's Day

This year, rather than buying a card from the store, why not make your loved ones a personalized Valentine's Day card? All you and/or your kids really need is imagination. but to get you started, consider the following:

• Look through a book of poetry to find just the right verse.

• Be brave and try expressing your thoughts directly.

• Take an 8½ x 11-inch piece of construction paper and fold in half. Keeping a ¼-inch margin at top and bottom of fold and between each design, cut little half hearts and other designs in the fold. Open up and voila! A homemade lace border.

• Decorate with lace doilies, glitter, dried flowers, bits of ribbon.

*Friends and
Family*

Christmas Creations

So often the little things that give comfort do so because of their recurrence in our lives—the sense of continuity we get from doing them over and over in exactly the same way. The world may be going to hell in a hand basket, but I enjoy that morning ritual of a cup of steaming black coffee no matter what.

That experience of coherence and connection was certainly the impetus for the annual Christmas cookie bake-off in my house each year when my stepchildren were growing up. Because they lived part-time with my husband and me and the rest of the time with their mother from the time that they were very young, they craved the little family ritual of the Christmas cookies, and wouldn't hear of skipping it. It is somewhat a labor-intensive process—first you must make the dough, roll it out, cut with cookie cutters (bells and Santas and reindeer of course) and bake. Then comes the cooling, the frosting and the decorating with all sorts of different color sugar sprinkles. It's a laborious operation for little ones and many a time I found myself alone in the kitchen, cursing the day I ever introduced them to the idea. But they would not hear of skipping, even one year. And when my stepdaughter went off to college and called me the week before Christmas to get the recipe—that was worth every Santa I had frosted over the past fourteen years.

"The pleasure of love is in loving."

—Le Rouchefoucauld

THINGS TO DO

The Best Christmas Cookies Ever

3 cups flour

½ teaspoon baking powder

⅛ teaspoon salt

1 cup butter or margarine

½ cup sugar

1 egg

2 teaspoons vanilla

Frosting

2 tablespoons hot water

1 cup confectioners' sugar

food coloring

chocolate sprinkles, cinnamon hearts, silver balls, red and green
sugar sprinkles or other edible decorations

    Preheat oven to 350 degrees. Sift flour, baking powder, and
salt in a medium bowl. In a large bowl, cream butter and sugar
together. Add egg and vanilla and beat until fluffy. Gradually stir
in sifted ingredients until well blended. Lightly flour a board.

213

*Friends and
Family*

With a floured rolling pin, roll small amount of dough ⅛-inch thick. Cut with Christmas cookie cutters, such as trees, Santas, bells, etc. Bake on ungreased cookie sheets until brown, about 10-12 minutes. Remove to rack to cool. Continue until dough is gone.

While cookies are cooling, make the frosting. Combine the hot water and sugar in a medium bowl. Divide the frosting into thirds. Color one with green food coloring, one with red, and leave the third white.

When cookies are cool, decorate with the frosting and add the various sprinkles. Let your imagination go wild! Makes 5 dozen.

A Thin Cat No More

We rescued our elderly cat from a lifetime of abuse and neglect, and when we first got him he weighed only eight pounds, smelled terrible, had mats in his fur, and all his bones stuck out. It's been one of the most wonderful experiences to watch him fill out to his natural weight of eighteen pounds, to see his fur grow in glossy and smooth, and to watch him change from a timid, clinging, frightened animal to who he is now: confident, friendly, regal. I love to bury my nose in his fur when he comes in—he smells like rain and fresh grass. But the best thing is to hold him (he likes to snuggle up facing me, like an infant) and to look into his eyes as he stares right back, and for a moment he and I understand each other perfectly. I can see his gratitude. He knows what has happened. He thanks me every day.

THINGS TO DO

An Easy Pick-Me-Up

When the winter doldrums really grip your family, how about hosting a slumber party for all your children's friends? They will love it and even if it provides a sleepless night for you, at least you won't be bored. To make it a night to remember, buy inexpensive plain pillowcases and have the kids sign them with permanent markers. Provide a variety of colors for artistic inspiration. Parents can later stitch over the names if they want and have a keepsake.

215

Friends and Family

A Grammarian's Fantasy

It's so nice to hear someone correctly use the subjunctive, as in "If I were a rich man." It's the thrill of rightness, of a job well done, of having someone show they take care of the language we all use. It's all we have to communicate with, and the more sloppily we use our language, the less clearly we communicate with one another. I also take pleasure in hearing someone use a particularly nice word in conversation—one that means exactly the right thing in the context in which it's used.

"Thought is the labor of the intellect, reverie is its pleasure."

—Victor Hugo

THINGS TO DO

The Dictionary Game

For people with a love of language and laughter, this is a hilarious game that can be played at home or in a car. All you need is a dictionary, pens, and pieces of paper. Here's how it works. Let's say you're "it". You pick a word that nobody in the game knows the meaning of. This is easier than you might think. Any dictionary is full of words that nobody has heard of. Words like "sirgang."

Once you've settled on a word, the game begins. You write out the exact dictionary definition, with all its variations, on a slip of paper. Don't show it to anyone. Meanwhile, everyone else writes down a made-up definition that sounds either deceptively legitimate or completely ridiculous—preferably both. The object is to imitate the dictionary style so well that you'll fool as many people as possible into believing yours is the real definition.

Once everybody has finished, they hand their paper to you, and you read out all the definitions, being careful to keep a straight face. This is easier said than done, because you'll end up reading definitions like sirgang: 1. carnivorous epiphyte native to Papua-New Guinea; 2. premium sirloin; (sl.) a cut above; 3. green Asian bird; 4. gathering of hoodlums who have achieved knighthood; 5. long strip of serge, wrapped around the waist and knotted at the side; 6. insulated wire used in electronic circuitry.

Each person except you then tries to guess the real definition; that's where the point system comes in. You get two points if nobody guesses the real meaning of the word you chose, and everyone else gets one point for each person who chooses his or her definition. The game continues till everyone has had a chance to be "it," and the points are totaled. (The person who chose definition #3 for "sirgang" is well on the way to winning.)

217

Friends and
Family

Brief Pleasures

The moment of recognition that comes when I pick up the
    phone and hear the voice of a dear friend I haven't spoken
    to for a long time.

The warmth in my chest as I gaze across a crowded room at the
    woman I love.

Slowing to walk after running really hard or really far, my body
    feeling relaxed to every fingertip as I realize there is noth-
    ing I would rather be doing in the whole world than walk-
    ing forward.

Pressing my face into a great green mound of moss in the winter
    woods and smelling a faint mysterious scent like cloves.

Sucking the golden crusty skin off a roasted marshmallow done
    to perfection over hot coals.

The politeness of a child to an elderly person when it's natural
    rather than dutiful.

The sound of a skipping rope solidly hitting the sidewalk during
    Double Dutch.

The milky smell of puppy breath, a little stinky but also sweet
with innocence.

The moment in tai chi when all my thoughts fade away and I no
longer feel like I'm doing a form, but the form is doing me.

Getting up very early in the morning to start on a road trip
before anyone's up, watching the sky grow rosy before
sunrise, smelling the dewy fields out the car window.

The cold nose of a dog pushed into your hand or face, and the
unconditional love that comes with it.

Hiding so well in hide-and-seek that no one ever finds you, and
the game ends and you're still hiding.

Remembering the name of somebody or something after it's
been on the tip of your tongue for days but wouldn't come
to you.

Being woken in the morning with butterfly kisses on the cheek.

⚲

How do you increase your happiness quotient?

We sincerely hope this book brings both pleasure and peace of mind into your life. We would love to know what Simple Pleasures you enjoy! Please mail us your favorite story and recipes for living well for our Simple Pleasures contest. The prize is an all-expense paid spa weekend for two for the best Simple Pleasure submitted. Here's to living happy, healthy lives!

Please mail your suggested Simple Pleasures *by December 31, 1997,* to:

Simple Pleasures Contest
Conari Press
2550 Ninth Street, Ste. 101
Berkeley, CA 94710

Index

223

Conari Press, established in 1987, publishes books on topics
ranging from spirituality and women's history to sexuality and
personal growth. Our main goal is to publish quality books
that will make a difference in people's lives—both
how we feel about ourselves and how
we relate to one another.

Our readers are our most important resource, and we
value your input, suggestions, and ideas. We'd love to hear
from you—after all, we are publishing
books for you!

For a complete catalog or to get on our mailing list,
please contact us at:

CONARI PRESS
2550 Ninth Street, Suite 101
Berkeley, CA 94710

800•685•9595   Fax 510•649•7190
e-mail: Conaripub@aol.com